New Members Training

The Lecture Series
Volume 9

Dr. Phil Fernandes
Institute of Biblical Defense

Bremerton, WA

New Members Training

Plus

Basic Christian Beliefs
Christian World View
(theology & apologetics)

Pastor Phil Fernandes

1

BASIC CHRISTIAN BELIEFS

The Bible

A) God's Word written in men's language (2 Timothy 3:16-17; 2 Peter 1:20-21).

B) Our only authority for faith and practice (Revelation 22:18-19; Proverbs 30:5-6; Ephesians 2:19-20).

C) God revealing Himself and His salvation to lost mankind (Isaiah 45:22; John 14:6).

God

A) God is spirit, He does not have a body (John 4:24; Colossians 1:15).

B) God is personal, He loves us (John 3:16).

C) God always existed (Psalm 90:2).

D) God is the Creator of all things (Genesis 1:1; John 1:1-3; Colossians 1:15-16).

E) There is only one God (Isaiah 43:10; 46:9).

F) The Father is God (Galatians 1:1).

G) The Son is God (John 1:1,14; Titus 2:13).

H) The Holy Spirit is God (Acts 5:3-4).

I) They are three separate Persons (Matthew 3:16-17; 28:19; John 14:26).

J) Definition of the Trinity- There is only one God, but in the unity of this one God there exists three separate Persons who are co-equal and co-eternal (see chart on the Trinity).

Jesus

A) Jesus is God (John 1:1,14; 10:30-33; Titus 2:13).

B) He was born of a virgin (Matthew 1:18-23).

C) He is fully-God and fully-man (Colossians 2:9).

D) He lived a sinless life (2 Corinthians 5:21).

E) He performed miracles (John 20:30-31).

F) He taught that salvation comes only through Him (John 14:6; 3:16-18).

G) He died for the sins of mankind (1 Peter 2:24; 3:18).

H) He rose from the dead (Matthew 28:1-10).

I) He appeared alive to many people after His death (1 Corinthians 15:3-8).

J) He ascended to heaven (Acts 1:9-11).

K) He sits at the Father's right hand (Hebrews 10:12).

L) He will someday return to earth (Matthew 24:29-31).

M) He will rule the earth for 1,000 years (Revelation 20:1-6).

N) He will rule the universe for all eternity (Revelation 11:15).

Salvation

A) All people are sinners (Romans 3:10, 23).

B) We cannot save ourselves (Matthew 19:25,26).

C) Jesus is the only way for us to be saved (John 14:6).

D) Jesus died for our sins; He took our punishment
   for us (1 Peter 2:24; 3:18).

E) We must trust in Him alone for salvation
   (John 3:16-18).

F) Those who trust Christ for salvation are "saved"
   and "born-again" (Ephesians 2:8-9; John 3:3;
   1 Peter 1:23).

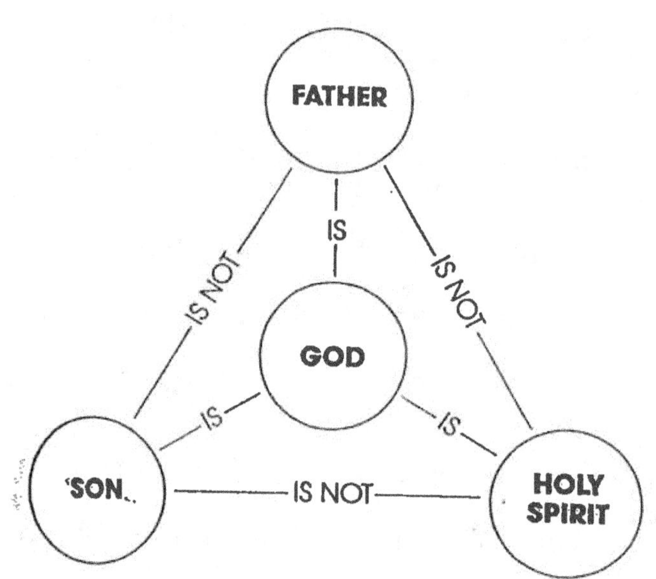

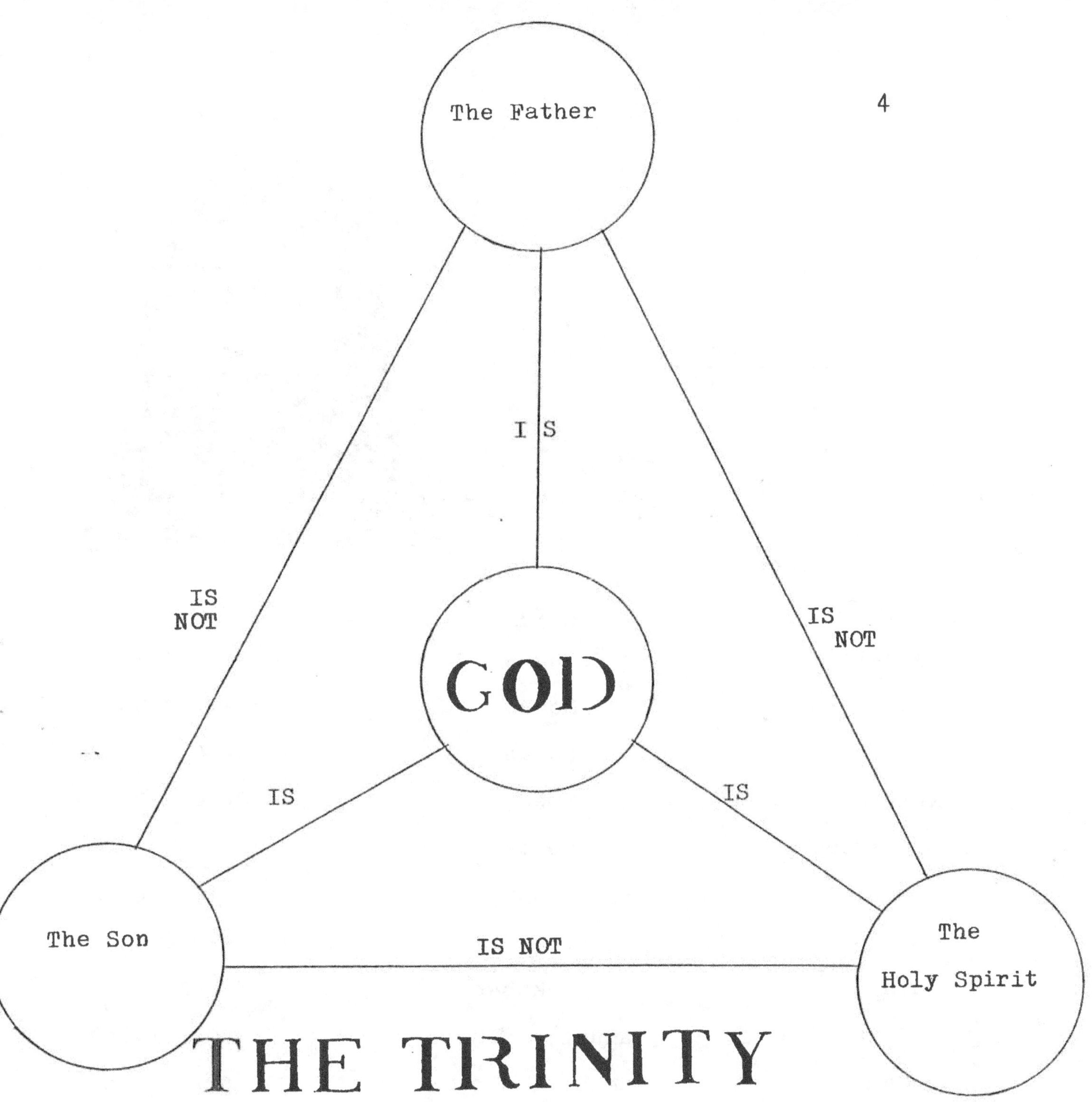

There is only one God, but in the unity of this one God there exists three separate Persons who are co-equal and co-eternal. This is called the doctrine of the Trinity.

2
BIBLE OVERVIEW

Old Testament Books

History	Author	Date
Genesis	Moses	1450-1410 BC
Exodus	Moses	1450-1410 BC
Leviticus	Moses	1450-1410 BC
Numbers	Moses	1450-1410 BC
Deuteronomy	Moses	1410 BC
Joshua	Joshua	1400-1370 BC
Judges	unknown	1050-1000 BC
Ruth	unknown	1000 BC
1 Samuel	Samuel & others	930 BC & later
2 Samuel	Samuel & others	930 BC & later
1 Kings	Jeremiah	550 BC
2 Kings	Jeremiah	550 BC
1 Chronicles	Ezra	450-425 BC
2 Chronicles	Ezra	450-425 BC
Ezra	Ezra	456-444 BC
Nehemiah	Nehemiah	445-425 BC
Esther	unknown	465 BC

Old Testament Books (continued)

Poetry	Author	Date
Job	unknown	unknown
Psalms	David & others	1,000 BC & later
Proverbs	Solomon & others	950-700 BC
Ecclesiastes	Solomon	935 BC
Song of Solomon	Solomon	965 BC

Prophecy	Author	Date
Isaiah	Isaiah	740-680 BC
Jeremiah	Jeremiah	627-585 BC
Lamentations	Jeremiah	586-585 BC
Ezekiel	Ezekiel	592-570 BC
Daniel	Daniel	537 BC
Hosea	Hosea	710 BC
Joel	Joel	835 BC
Amos	Amos	755 BC
Obadiah	Obadiah	840 or 586 BC
Jonah	Jonah	760 BC
Micah	Micah	700 BC
Nahum	Nahum	663-612 BC
Habbakuk	Habbakuk	607 BC
Zephaniah	Zephaniah	625 BC
Haggai	Haggai	520 BC
Zechariah	Zechariah	520-518 BC
Malachi	Malachi	450-400 BC

New Testament Books

History	Author	Date
Matthew	Matthew	60's AD
Mark	Mark	50's AD
Luke	Luke	60 AD
John	John	85-90 AD
Acts	Luke	61 AD

Letters	Author	Date
Romans	Paul	58 AD
1 Corinthians	Paul	56 AD
2 Corinthians	Paul	57 AD
Galatians	Paul	49 or 55 AD
Ephesians	Paul	61 AD
Philippians	Paul	61 AD
Colossians	Paul	61 AD
1 Thessalonians	Paul	51 AD
2 Thessalonians	Paul	51 AD
1 Timothy	Paul	63 AD
2 Timothy	Paul	66 AD
Titus	Paul	65 AD
Philemon	Paul	61 AD
Hebrews	unknown	64-68 AD
James	James	45-50 AD
1 Peter	Peter	63 AD
2 Peter	Peter	66 AD
1 John	John	90 AD

<u>New Testament Books</u> (continued)

<u>Letters</u> (continued)	<u>Author</u>	<u>Date</u>
2 John	John	90 AD
3 John	John	90 AD
Jude	Jude	70-80 AD
<u>Prophecy</u>	<u>Author</u>	<u>Date</u>
Revelation	John	90's AD

<u>Bible History</u>

A) <u>Creation Period</u> (ancient history of human race)

    1) creation

    2) fall

    3) flood

    4) tower

    5) Genesis 1-11

    6) 4004-2165 BC

B) <u>Patriarch Period</u> (start of the Hebrew nation)

    1) Abraham

    2) Isaac

    3) Jacob

    4) Joseph & eleven brothers (12 tribes)

    5) Job

    6) Genesis 11-50; Job

    7) 2165-1804 BC

C) <u>Exodus Period</u>

    1) Moses & wilderness wandering after release from Egypt

    2) Exodus, Leviticus, Numbers, Deuteronomy

    3) 1804-1382 BC

D) <u>Conquest Period</u> (Joshua & taking the promised land)

    1) Joshua

    2) 1405-1382 BC

E) <u>Judges Period</u> (13 Judges of Israel)

    1) Judges, Ruth, 1 Samuel 1-7

    2) 1382-1043 BC

F) <u>United Kingdom Period</u>

    1) Saul, David, Solomon

    2) 1 Samuel 8-31; 2 Samuel, 1 Kings 1-11; 1 Chronicles, 2 Chronicles 1-9; Psalms, Proverbs, Ecclesiastes; Song of Solomon

    3) 1043-931 BC

G) <u>Divided Kingdom Period</u>

    1) 10 northen tribes split with the 2 southern tribes

    2) 10 northen tribes taken captive by Assyria afterwards

    3) 1 Kings 12-22; 2 Kings; 2 Chronicles 10-36; Obadiah; Joel; Jonah; Amos; Hosea; Isaiah; Micah; Nahum; Zephaniah; Jeremiah; Habakkuk; Lamentations

    4) 931-605 BC

H) <u>Captivity Period</u> (2 southern tribes under Babylon rule)

    1) Daniel, Ezekiel

    2) 605-538 BC

I) <u>Return Period</u> (2 southern tribes under Medo-Persian rule)

    1) Jews allowed to return to Holy Land

    2) Ezra; Esther; Nehemiah; Haggai; Zechariah; Malachi

    3) 538-400 BC

J) <u>400 Silent Years</u> (no Books of the Bible written)

    1) 400 year gap between Old & New Testaments

    2) Jews under Greek rule (later, under Roman rule)

    3) 400-5 BC

K) <u>Gospel Period</u> (the life of Jesus the Jewish Messiah)

    1) under Roman rule (323 BC-476 AD)

    2) Matthew; Mark; Luke; John

    3) 5BC-30AD

L) <u>Early Church Period</u> (gospel spreads over the world)

    1) Peter, Paul

    2) Acts

    3) 30 AD - 60 AD

M) <u>The Epistles</u> (apostolic letters teaching Christians
how to live Godly lives)

    1) Romans, 1 & 2 Corinthians; Galatians, Ephesians;
Philippians; Colossians; 1 & 2 Thessalonians;
1 & 2 Timothy; Titus; Philemon; Hebrews; James;
1 & 2 Peter; 1 & 2 & 3 John; Jude; Revelation

    2) 45 AD - 100 AD

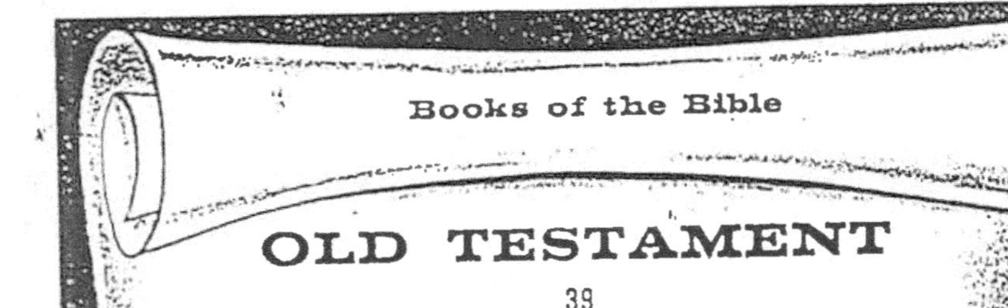

Books of the Bible

OLD TESTAMENT
39

HISTORY

THE PENTATEUCH (Books of Moses or of the Law) (5)
Genesis   Leviticus   Deuteronomy
Exodus   Numbers
THE HISTORICAL BOOKS (12)
Joshua   Second Samuel   Second Chronicles
Judges   First Kings   Ezra
Ruth   Second Kings   Nehemiah
First Samuel   First Chronicles   Esther

POETRY

THE POETICAL and WISDOM BOOKS (5)
Job   Proverbs   Song of Solomon
Psalms   Ecclesiastes

PROPHECY

THE MAJOR PROPHETS (5)
Isaiah   Lamentations   Daniel
Jeremiah   Ezekiel
THE MINOR PROPHETS (12)
Hosea   Obadiah   Nahum   Haggai
Joel   Jonah   Habakkuk   Zechariah
Amos   Micah   Zephaniah   Malachi

Books of the Bible

NEW TESTAMENT
27

HISTORY

THE GOSPELS (4)
Matthew   Luke
Mark   John
THE BOOK of ACTS (1)

EPISTLES

THE PAULINE EPISTLES (13)
Romans   Colossians
First Corinthians   First Thessalonians
Second Corinthians   Second Thessalonians
Galatians   First Timothy
Ephesians   Second Timothy
Philippians   Titus
              Philemon
THE GENERAL EPISTLES (8)
Hebrews   First John
James   Second John
First Peter   Third John
Second Peter   Jude

PROPHECY

THE BOOK of REVELATION (1)

3

SPIRIT-FILLED LIVING

Obedience

A) we are not under the law; we are under grace (Romans 6:14).

B) Christianity is not a list of rules and regulations (Galatians 2:21).

C) Christianity is a personal relationship with Christ (John 5:39-40).

D) we obey God...

    1) by our love for God and men (Mark 12:30-31; Romans 13:10; John 14:15).

    2) by our faith and trust in Jesus for guidance (Romans 3:31; 14:23).

Prayer (communication with God)

A) Jesus is our only mediator with God, we don't pray to saints (1 Timothy 2:5).

B) Pray for God's will, not your own (Matthew 6:9-10; 26:39; James 4:3; 4:13-16; 1 John 5:14-15).

C) Praying in Jesus' Name means praying for Jesus' will (John 6:38; 5:43).

D) When we are in God's will, He answers our prayers (John 15:7).

E) Delight yourself in the Lord, He'll give you the desires of your heart (Psalm 37:4).

F) Pray without ceasing (1 Thessalonians 5:17).

<u>Trials and Discipline</u>

A) <u>Trials</u> - when God allows obedient Christians to
suffer to cause them to spiritually
grow. (James 1:2-4; Job)

B) <u>Discipline</u> - when God punishes a disobedient
Christian. (1 Corinthians 11:32;
Hebrews 12:5-6; Jonah)

<u>Fruit of the Spirit</u> (Galatians 5:22-23)

A) all believers are indwelt by the Holy Spirit and
have access to this fruit.

B) still, we can suppress the Holy Spirit from bring-
ing this fruit out of us.

C) the fruit displayed in a believer's life shows the
spiritual maturity level of the believer.

D) the fruit of the Spirit

1) love

2) joy

3) peace

4) patience

5) kindness

6) goodness

7) faithfulness

8) gentleness

9) self-control

<u>The Gifts of the Spirit</u>

A) 1 Corinthians 12:4-10; Romans 12:6-7; Ephesians 4:11-12;
1 Peter 4:10-11

B) supernatural abilities given to us by the Holy Spirit
(1 Corinthians 12:11).

C) purpose- to help strengthen the church (1 Corinthians
12:7; 14:26).

D) not a sign of maturity (1 Corinthians 1:7; 3:1)

E) if practised without love, gifts are useless.
   fruit is a sign of spiritual maturity (1 Corinthians 13:1-3).

F) gifts must be used orderly (1 Corinthians 14:39-40).

G) should not force others to have our gifts (1 Corinthians 12:29-30).

H) all believers are baptized with the Holy Spirit
   (Matthew 3:11-12).

I) all believers have spiritual gifts (1 Corinthians
   12:13).

J) which gifts do you have ? (God will use your gifts
   to enable you to perform the ministry He has for you).

   1) word of wisdom-the supernatural insight into
      the true nature of things so that one is able
      to discern the right course of action to take.

   2) word of knowledge-a supernatural understanding
      of a particular situation.

   3) faith-not saving faith, but a supernatural
      and perfect reliance on God.

   4) healing-the ability to heal, cure, or to
      make whole. (it is not always God's will
      to heal).

   5) miracles-the ability to perform supernatural
      works of power.

   6) prophecy-to proclaim a message from God.
      not always futuristic. (direction, not
      doctrine).

   7) distinguishing of spirits-the ability to dis-
      cern whether something is from God or not.

   8) tongues-the ability to speak in an unknown
      language (human or angelic).

   9) interpretation of tongues-the ability to inter-
      pret the unknown language spoken by another.

   10) service-the ability to humbly serve, help, or
       minister to others. (wait on tables)

   11) teaching-the ability to give instruction to
       others so that they learn from you and grow spiritually.

12) exhortation-the ability to stand by someone and encourage them. (point to joy)

13) mercy showing-the ability to show compassion for someone. (cry with them)

14) giving-the ability to share of one's time, talent, or treasure.

15) leading-the ability to guide others along the path.

16) apostleship-one sent forth with a message and the authority of the one who sent him. (those commissioned directly by Christ) no longer a gift today.

17) evangelism-the ability to lead others to Christ by proclaiming the Good News.

18) pastor-teacher-the ability to not only instruct the flock but to shepherd them by tending to their needs and protecting them from false teachers.

19) speaking-the ability to speak in such a manner that you are easily understood and able to keep the attention of others.

4

CHURCH LIFE

Universal Church (all true believers)

A) Matthew 16:15-18

B) universal church is built on a person's confession of Christ as God and Savior.

Local Church (Romans 16:3-5)

Functions of the Church

A) evangelism (Matthew 28:19-20)

B) Biblical instruction (Matthew 28:20)

C) ordinances (water baptism & Lord's supper-Acts 2:41-42, this verse contains all 5 functions)

D) worship & prayer (Ephesians 5:18-20)

E) fellowship (Hebrews 10:23-25; 1 John 1:3)

Water Baptism

A) does not save; done in obedience to Christ's command (Matthew 28:19)

B) baptizo-to dip or fully submerge

C) symbolizes our identification with Christ in His death, burial, and resurrection (Romans 6:3-6)

D) symbolizes the death of the old man and the birth of the new man (2 Corinthians 5:17)

E) water baptism is the outward sign of the inward
work of the Holy Spirit (Spirit Baptism-1 Corinthians 12:13)

F) baptism is a public confession of a person's
faith in Christ (Matthew 10:32-33)

G) baptism is done in the name of the Triune God
(Matthew 28:19)

1) public confession   2) death & burial   3) resurrection
   of Christ   of the old man   of the new man

Lord's Supper (1 Corinthians 11:23-26)

A) done in remembrance of the Lord's death (a memorial)

B) to be practised until He returns

C) symbolic of our coming to Christ & believing in Him
(John 6:35)

D) symbolic of the church being the Body of Christ
(1 Corinthians 10:16-17)

E) Catholic View-bread and wine become the literal
body and blood of Christ; Christ is resacrificed
each Mass. (false-Hebrews 10:10-14; John 6:35)

F) Biblical View-bread and wine symbolize the body
and blood of Christ; we celebrate the Lord's Supper
as a memorial to Christ's sacrificial death on
Calvary.

G) God disciplines believers who partake of the Lord's
Supper in an unworthy manner. (1 Corinthians 11:27-34)

<u>Stewardship</u> (our managing the estate that God has
                entrusted to us-our time, talent, and
                treasure)

A) <u>tithing</u> (giving 10% of our income to God's work)

    1) Malachi 3:8-10

    2) Proverbs 3:9-10

    3) Luke 6:38

    4) 2 Corinthians 9:6-7

    5) tithing was practised before the Law came
       into effect (Hebrews 7:9-10)

B) <u>the need</u>

    1) support of local church (1 Corinthians 9:14)

    2) other Christians in need (1 Corinthians 16:1-3)

    3) aid for the helpless poor, not the lazy
       (James 1:27; 2 Thessalonians 3:10)

    4) to finance the spreading of the Gospel
       (Luke 9:1-6; 10:1-11)

<u>Church Discipline</u>

A) proper procedure (Matthew 18:15-17)

B) Biblical examples (1 Corinthians 5:1-13; 1 Timothy
   1:18-20; Romans 16:17)

5

FAMILY LIFE

Number One Ministry

1 Timothy 4:4-5; 5:8

Marriage (Matthew 19:3-6)

A) two become one

B) life-long committment

C) Biblical ideal- one man, one woman, one lifetime

Role of Husband/Father

A) provide for family (1 Timothy 4:4-5; 5:8)

B) love wife as Christ loves the Church (Ephesians 5:25; Colossians 3:19)

C) properly discipline children (Proverbs 22:6; 19:18; 13:24; Ephesians 6:4; Colossians 3:21; Proverbs 18:19)

Role of Wife/Mother

A) submit to husband's leadership (Ephesians 5:24; Colossians 3:18)

B) responsibilities-housework, but may also work outside home (Titus 2:3-5; Proverbs 31:10, 16, 30)

Role of Children (Ephesians 6:1-3; Colossians 3:20; Proverbs 12:1; 13:1). obey parents & accept discipline

<u>Work Performance</u>

A) work (2 Thessalonians 3:10)

B) work hard (Proverbs 14:23)

C) work as if for the Lord (Colossians 3:23)

D) use money wisely (Ecclesiastes 11:2)

6

*STUDYING THE WORD

Hear

A) Romans 10:17

B) we need to hear the Word properly preached by someone grounded in the Word. This will increase our faith.

Read

A) Revelation 1:3; Acts 17:11

B) we need to read the Word on our own to receive God's blessings and to test what others are teaching us.

Study

A) 2 Timothy 2:15

B) we must study the Word to handle it accurately

C) concordances, Bible encyclopedias, commentaries, study Bibles, maps, other reference works

Memorize

A) Psalm 119:11; Matthew 4:1-4, 7, 10

B) to know God's Word we should also memorize key verses that will comfort us in our time of need and aid us in resisting temptation. We should also use these verses to counsel others.

<u>Meditate</u>

A) Joshua 1:8; Psalm 119:15,27,97

B) <u>false meditation</u>-emptying one's mind, allowing demonic influences to set in.

C) <u>Biblical meditation</u>-emptying one's mind of selfish desires and filling one's mind with principles from God's Word and reflecting on these principles.

* this study is taken from the Navigator studies

Religion	View of God	View of Jesus	View of Salvation
Christianity	One personal God One God, three persons	fully God & fully man; died on cross for our sins; rose from the dead	By grace alone Through faith alone In Jesus alone
Judaism	One personal God	Merely a man	Devotion to God; obedience to His commands (OT)
Islam	One personal God	A great prophet; not as great as Muhammad	Devotion to God; obedience to His commands (Koran)
Hinduism	God is a non-personal force; God is the universe; Man is God	One of many manifestations of God	Eastern meditation Reincarnation Follow guru Self-deification
Buddhism	Agnostic in regards to God's existence	A great moral teacher	4 noble truths 8-fold path
Secular Humanism	No god	Merely a man	No life after death
New Age Movement	God is a non-personal force; God is the universe; man is God	One of the many manifestations of God	Self-deification; reincarnation; meditation; guru; new age on earth
Bahai Faith	One God who is revealed in all the world's religions	One of the many manifestations of God	Devotion to God; faithfulness to one of the world's religions
Mormonism	Many gods; Mormon males can become gods someday	Not always God; became a god; is getting better as God	Faith in the Mormon Jesus; Mormon baptism; obey Mormon commands; eternal progression
Jehovah's Witnesses	One personal God; deny Trinity	A lesser god; the first creation; He created everything else	Faith in the JW Jesus; obedience to God's Laws

Basic Christian Beliefs
Pastor Phil Fernandes

1) The Trinity
- A) there is only one God (Isa 43:10; 44:6; 46:9; 1 Tm 2:5)
- B) the Father is God (Gal 1:1; 1 Pt 1:1-2)
- C) the Son is God (Titus 2:13; Jn 1:1, 14; 2 Pt 1:1; Jn 5:17-18; 8:58-59; 10:30-33)
- D) the Holy Spirit is God (Acts 5:3-4; 1 Cor 3:16)
- E) they are three distinct Persons (Mt 3:16-17; Jon 14:16, 26)
- F) there is only one true God, but this God exists throughout all eternity as three equal Persons

2) Creation by God
- A) God created everything else out of nothing (ex nihilo)
- B) Gen 1:1; Jn 1:1-3; Col 1:15-17
- C) evidence for God (origin of universe, design, morality, reason, free will, human rights, guilt, meaning, defeat of evil)
- D) unproven assumptions of evolution
    1) something from nothing
    2) life from non-life
    3) multi-celled animals from single-celled animals
    4) animals with backbones from animals without backbones
    5) the common ancestry of fish, reptiles, birds, mammals, & man (could be common design)
- E) evolution itself is an unproven assumption

3) The Bible is God's Inerrant Word
- A) 2 Tm 3:16-17; 2 Pt 1:20-21; Prov 30:5-6; Jn 17:17
- B) revelation = God revealed His word to human authors
- C) inspiration = God guided human authors to record His

Word totally without error
D) <u>canonization</u> = God guided the early church to recognize
    which books belong in the New Testament
E) <u>authority</u> = the Bible is the final authority for faith &
    Morality (Sola Scriptura)

4) Man is Fallen and Sinful; we cannot save ourselves
A) we inherited Adam's sin nature (Rm 5:12)
B) Rm 3:10, 23; Mt 19:25-26; Jn 3:3

5) Salvation by Grace alone through Faith alone in Jesus alone
A) salvation is a free gift of God given to those who trust in
    Jesus alone for salvation; Sola Gratia & Sola Fide;
    (Eph 2:8-9; Jn 14:6; Acts 4:12; Jn 3:16-18)
B) ~~you can't have the Father if you reject the Son~~
    (1 Jn 2:23; Lk 10:16; Mt 10:32-33)
C) Christians don't do good works to get saved; we do good
    works because we are saved
D) good works are not the cause of salvation; good works are
    the result of salvation (Eph 2:10)
E) true saving faith produces good works (Jm 2:26; Rm 3:31)

6) The Deity of Christ—Jesus is God the Son
A) Jesus is God the Son (Col 2:9; 2 Pt 1:1; Php 2:5-6;
    Jn 5:22-23; 8:23-24, 58-59; 10:30-33; 17:5; 20:28;
    Mt 12:6, 8, 42; Mt 28:20)
B) Jesus called God His "Abba" (Jn 5:17-18;
C) Jesus claimed the power to forgive sin (Mk 2:5-7)
D) His truly, truly statements (Mt 5:21-22)
E) Old Testament prophecies call Jesus Elohim or Yahweh
    (Isa 7:14; 9:6; Jer 23:5-6; Zech 14:5)
E) <u>the incarnation</u> = God the Son became a man (Jn 1:1, 14)
F) <u>hypostatic union</u> = Jesus is one Person with two natures
    forever; He is fully God and fully man (Titus 2:13;
    1 Tm 2:5)

G) <u>the kenosis</u> = Jesus veiled His glory & humbled Himself
        by becoming a man; He did not use certain attributes to
        His advantage (Php 2:5-11; Mk 13:32)

7) <u>The Virgin Birth—God the Son became a man</u>
        --Jesus had no earthly father; He was born to the virgin Mary
        (Isa 7:14; Mt 1:18-25; Lk 1:35)

8) <u>The Substitutionary Death of Christ</u>
        A) Jesus died on the cross for our sins (1 Cor 15:3; Jn 1:29;
                Mt 1:21; 2 Cor 5:15))
        B) He took our punishment for us & died in our place
                (1 Pt 2:24; 3:18; 2 Cor 5:21; 1 Cor 5:7)
        C) He defeated Satan and His demons (Col 2:13-15)
        D) He paid the price for our sins to the Father's justice, not to
                Satan; God owes Satan nothing (Mk 10:45; 1 Cor 6:20)
        E) He did not merely set a good example for us

9) <u>Jesus' Bodily Resurrection</u>
        A) Jesus conquered death for us by rising from the dead
                (1 Cor 15:32, 55-57)
        B) the Father accepted the Son's sacrifice
        C) the importance of the resurrection (1 Cor 15:14, 17)
        D) the resurrection is an essential part of the Gospel
                (1 Cor 15:1-8; Rm 10:9)
        E) Christ's resurrection was bodily (Jn 2:19-21; 20:24-29;
                Lk 24:36-43)

10) <u>Jesus' Future Return to Earth</u>
        A) Jesus will return in the last days (Rev 1:7; Jn 14:1-3)
        B) after the tribulation period (Mt 24:29-31; Rev 19:11-16)
        C) He will reign on earth for 1,000 years (Rev 20)

Different Views of God

1) <u>pantheism</u> = God is the universe; God is non-personal
2) <u>polytheism</u> = many gods
3) <u>dualism</u> = two competing gods
4) <u>panentheism</u> = the universe is god's body
5) <u>finite theism</u> = a god who is limited in power
6) <u>atheism</u> = no God
7) <u>agnosticism</u> = man cannot know God
8) <u>deism</u> = a God who cannot or does not perform miracles
9) <u>theism</u> = the true view; one personal God who created the
     universe and is separate from the universe, but is involved
     with the universe (He can perform miracles)

The Attributes or Characteristics of God

1) <u>good</u> (Matthew 19:17)
2) <u>eternal</u> = no beginning & no end (Psalm 90:2)
3) <u>omnipresent</u> = everywhere present (Psalm 139:7-8)
4) <u>omnipotent</u> = all-powerful (Matthew 19:25-26)
5) <u>omniscient</u> = all-knowing (Psalm 147:5)
6) <u>immutable</u> = never changes (Hebrews 13:8; 1:10-12)
7) <u>sovereign</u> = always in control (Isaiah 46:9-11)
8) <u>holy</u> = totally separate from evil; absolutely pure
     (1 Peter 1:14-16)
9) <u>righteous</u> = His deeds are just (2 Timothy 4:7-8)
10) <u>true</u> = He cannot lie (1 Samuel 15:29; John 14:6)
11) <u>faithful</u> = absolutely loyal (1 Thessalonians 5:24)
12) <u>merciful</u> = spares us the punishment we deserve
     (Ephesians 2:4)
13) <u>gracious</u> = unmerited favor; gives us the salvation we don't
     deserve (Ephesians 2:8-9)
14) <u>loving</u> = unconditional seeking the highest good for others
     (John 3:16; 1 John 4:8)

Christian World View

Instructor: Dr. Phil Fernandes

P. O. Box 3264
Bremerton, WA 98310
(360) 698-7382

copyright 2002

Christian World View

Part 1

Theology

The Study of God

Bible Doctrines

The Christian World View

1)<u>Creation</u> (Genesis 1:1, 27, 31: 2:25; 9:6)
    A)human life is sacred
    B)God created a perfect world
    C)we corrupted the world by sinning
2)<u>Fall</u> (Genesis 3:7; Romans 5:12; 3:10, 23)
    A)we are all fallen sinners
    B)we cannot save ourselves
    C)limited government—serves man; does not
        enslave him
3)<u>Redemption</u> (John 3:16-18; 14:6; 1:29)
    A)only Jesus, through His death & resurrection,
        can save us
    B)there is no other hope for mankind
4)<u>Restoration</u> (Romans 8:18-25; 1 Corinthians 15:50-
    58; Revelation 11:15; 21:1-4; Matthew 5:13-16)
        A)we can make the world a better place
        B)we cannot make it perfect
        C)only Jesus can make it perfect
        D)the Kingdom of God
            1)present, spiritual stage (Rm 14:17)
            2)future, physical stage (Rev 11:15)

***suggested reading—_How Shall We Now Live_
                By Chuck Colson & Nancy Pearcy

INSTITUTE OF BIBLICAL DEFENSE

P. O. Box 3264, Bremerton, WA. 98310 * (360) 698-7382
Dr. Phil Fernandes, President

BASIC CHRISTIAN BELIEFS

1) The Trinity
    A) Only one God (Isa 43:10; 44:6; 46:9; 1 Tm 2:5)
    B) Father is God (Gal 1:1; 1 Pt 1:1-2)
    C) Son is God (Ti 2:13; Jn 1:1,14; 2 Pt 1:1; Jn 8:58-59; 10:30-33)
    D) Holy Spirit is God (Acts 5:3-4; 1 Cor 3:16)
    E) They are 3 separate Persons (Mt 3:16-17; Jn 14:16, 26)

2) Creation by God (Gen 1:1; Jn 1:1-3; Col 1:15-16)

3) Biblical Inspiration & Inerrancy (2 Tm 3:16-17; 2 Pt 1:20-21;
    Prov 30:5-6; Jn 17:17; Jude 3; Eph 2:19-20)

4) Salvation by Grace through Faith in Christ Alone (Eph 2:8-9;
    Jn 14:6; Acts 4:12; Rm 3:10,23; Mt 19:25-26; Jn 3:16-18;
    1 Jn 2:23; Lk 10:16; Jm 2:26)

5) The Virgin Birth of Christ (Isa 7:14; Mt 1:18-25; Lk 1:35)

6) The Deity of Christ (Col 2:9; Jn 1:1,14; Ti 2:13; 2 Pt 1:1; Philip-
    pians 2:5-6; Jn 5:17-18, 22-23; 8:23-24, 58-59; 10:30-33; 20:28)

7) The Bodily Resurrection of Christ (Rm 10:9; 1 Cor 15:3-8,14,17;
    Jn 2:19-21; 20:24-29; Lk 24:36-43)

8) The Bodily, Visible Return of Christ (Rev 1:7; Jn 14:1-3; Mt 24:
    29-31; Rev 19:11-16)

9) The Substitutionary Death of Christ (1 Pt 2:24; 3:18; 2 Cor 5:21;
    1 Cor 5:7; Jn 1:29; Mt 1:21; 2 Cor 5:15)

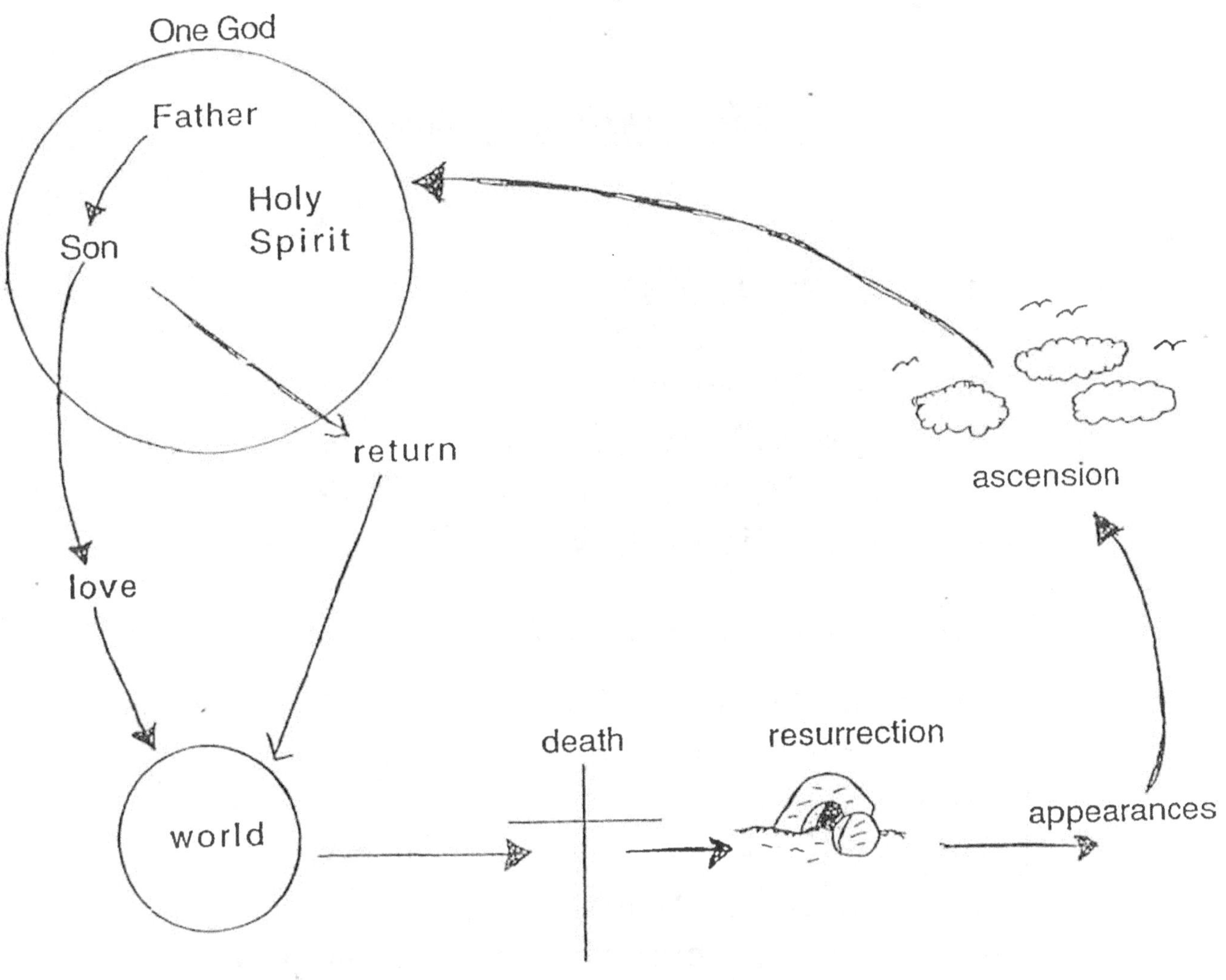

<u>10 Gospel Truths</u>
1) only one God
2) God is 3 Persons
3) God the Father loves the world
4) God the Father sent His Son into the world
5) God's Son became a man
6) He died on the cross for our sins
7) He rose from the dead on the third day
8) He appeared to His disciples
9) He ascended to heaven
10) He will return someday

<u>Our Threefold Response</u>
1) admit we are sinners & we cannot save ourselves
2) trust in Jesus alone for salvation
3) trust in Jesus & His Word for daily living

Theological Issues

1) The Christian World View
   - A) basic Christian beliefs
   - B) the Gospel Diagram
   - C) the Christian View of God
     - --His existence, nature, & attributes
   - D) statement of faith (KW & IBD)

2) Issues World Views Must Explain
   - A) evil & human suffering
   - B) moral laws (moral responsibility)
   - C) truth
   - D) origin of universe
   - E) design & order in universe
   - F) strange events (miracles, UFO's, hauntings)
   - G) source of authority (gov't, ultimate authority?)
   - H) meaning in life

3) Tests World Views Must Pass
   - A) logical consistency (no contradictions)
   - B) correspond to reality
   - C) explanatory power
   - D) livable
   - E) more plausible than other world views?
   - F) cultural impact (good or bad?)

The IBD Statement of Faith

GOD—There is only one God. This one God eternally exists as three equal Persons (Father, Son, and Holy Spirit). This one God is the all-powerful, all-knowing, everywhere-present Creator and Sustainer of the universe. This one God is loving, just, good, holy, true, faithful, gracious, merciful, sovereign, and eternal. The triune God is infinite in all His attributes.

JESUS—Jesus Christ was always God and will always be God, the second Person of the Trinity. Without ceasing to be God, He became a man when He was born of a virgin. He lived a sinless and miraculous life, died on the cross for our sins (taking our punishment upon Himself), and bodily rose from the dead to conquer death for us. Jesus ascended to heaven, sits enthroned at the Father's right hand, and will someday visibly return to judge the living and the dead. Jesus will bring God's Kingdom to earth and reign on the earth for 1,000 years. After the millennial reign, Jesus will establish the new heavens and the new earth, and reign over the universe forever. Jesus is the Jewish Messiah (the one anointed by God to rescue Israel) and the Savior of mankind.

SALVATION—Salvation is by God's grace alone, and we accept this free gift of salvation through faith alone in Jesus alone as our God and Savior. Salvation cannot be earned—we are all sinners who deserve the eternal flames of hell. Though we are not saved by works, genuine faith produces good works in our lives.

BIBLE—The Bible is the inspired Word of God, recorded in its original manuscripts totally without error. The Scriptures are profitable for the teaching of the redeemed in doctrine as well as in daily living. The Bible is the final authority upon which all other things are to be tested.

<u>Christian World View-Bible 11</u>
Dr. Fernandes

1)<u>True Spirituality</u>
    A)propositional truth + personal relationship
    B)John 4:24
    C)we must know the true doctrines about Jesus &
        salvation
    D)we must enter into a personal relationship with
        the true Jesus of the Bible
2)<u>Bible Doctrines (Theology)</u>
    A)Theology Proper (Doctrine of God)
    B)Christology (Doctrine of Christ)
    C)Pneumatology (Doctrine of the Holy Spirit)
    D)Anthropology (Doctrine of Man)
    E)Hamartiology (Doctrine of Sin)
    F)Soteriology (Doctrine of Salvation)
    G)Angelology (Doctrine of Angels)
    H)Demonology (Doctrine of Demons)
    I)Satanology (Doctrine of Satan)
    J)Eschatology (Doctrine of the End Times)
    K)Ecclesiology (Doctrine of the Church)
    L)Bibliology (Doctrine of the Bible)
3)<u>Biblical Defense (Apologetics)</u>
    A)Creation Science
    B)Refuting Non-Christian World Views
    C)Evidence for God
    D)Old Testament Reliability
    E)New Testament Reliability
    F)Evidence for Christ's Resurrection
    G)Evidence for Christ's Deity
    H)Evidence the Bible is God's Word
    I)Refuting Moral Relativism

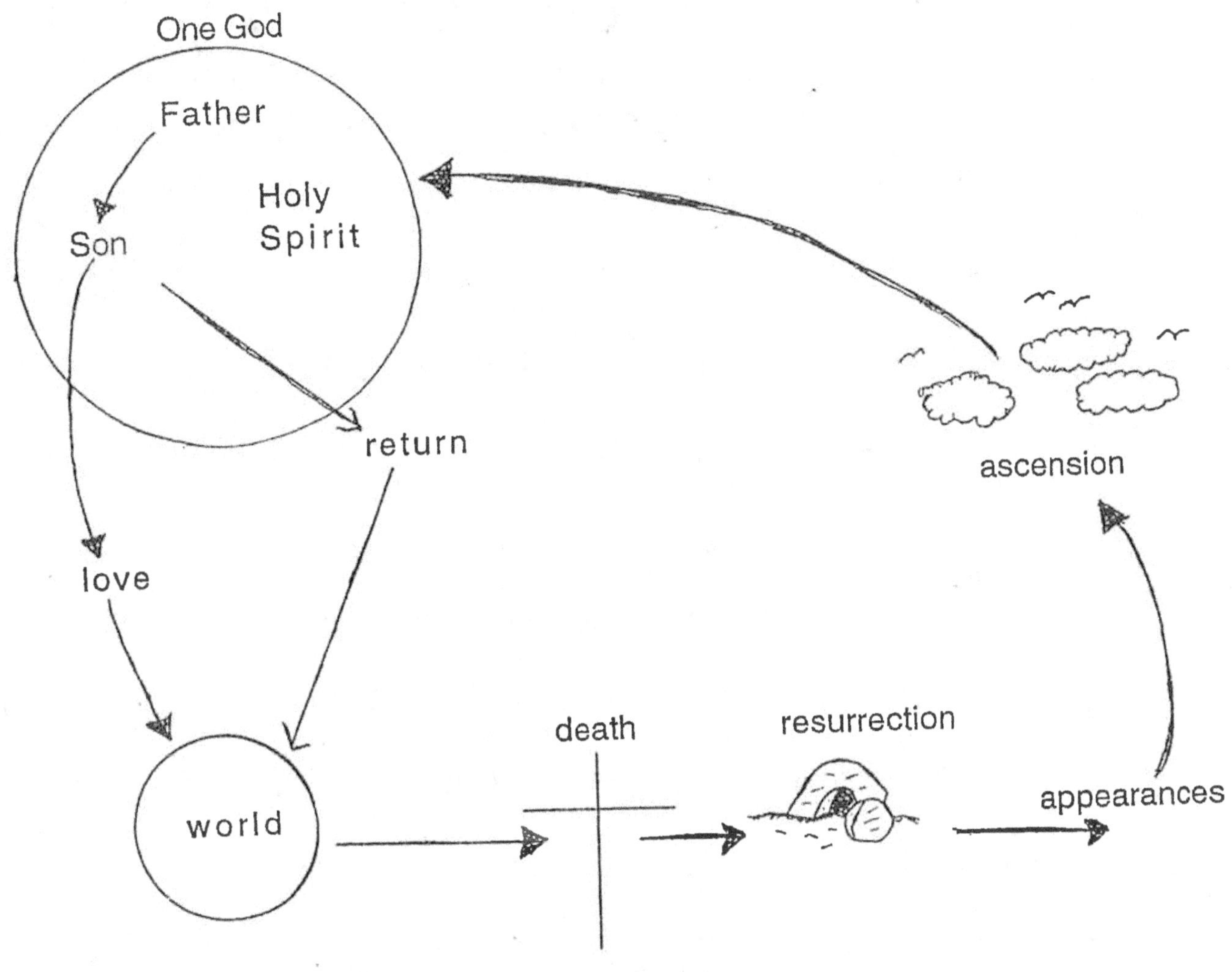

10 Gospel Truths

1) only one God
2) God is 3 Persons
3) God the Father loves the world
4) God the Father sent His Son into the world
5) God's Son became a man
6) He died on the cross for our sins
7) He rose from the dead on the third day
8) He appeared to His disciples
9) He ascended to heaven
10) He will return someday

Our Threefold Response

1) admit we are sinners & we cannot save ourselves
2) trust in Jesus alone for salvation
3) trust in Jesus & His Word for daily living

INSTITUTE OF BIBLICAL DEFENSE

P. O. Box 3264, Bremerton, WA. 98310 * (360) 698-7382
Dr. Phil Fernandes, President

BASIC CHRISTIAN BELIEFS

1) The Trinity
    A) Only one God (Isa 43:10; 44:6; 46:9; 1 Tm 2:5)
    B) Father is God (Gal 1:1; 1 Pt 1:1-2)
    C) Son is God (Ti 2:13; Jn 1:1,14; 2 Pt 1:1; Jn 8:58-59; 10:30-33)
    D) Holy Spirit is God (Acts 5:3-4; 1 Cor 3:16)
    E) They are 3 separate Persons (Mt 3:16-17; Jn 14:16, 26)

2) Creation by God (Gen 1:1; Jn 1:1-3; Col 1:15-16)

3) Biblical Inspiration & Inerrancy (2 Tm 3:16-17; 2 Pt 1:20-21;
    Prov 30:5-6; Jn 17:17; Jude 3; Eph 2:19-20)

4) Salvation by Grace through Faith in Christ Alone (Eph 2:8-9;
    Jn 14:6; Acts 4:12; Rm 3:10,23; Mt 19:25-26; Jn 3:16-18;
    1 Jn 2:23; Lk 10:16; Jm 2:26)

5) The Virgin Birth of Christ (Isa 7:14; Mt 1:18-25; Lk 1:35)

6) The Deity of Christ (Col 2:9; Jn 1:1,14; Ti 2:13; 2 Pt 1:1; Philip-
    pians 2:5-6; Jn 5:17-18, 22-23; 8:23-24, 58-59; 10:30-33; 20:28)

7) The Bodily Resurrection of Christ (Rm 10:9; 1 Cor 15:3-8,14,17;
    Jn 2:19-21; 20:24-29; Lk 24:36-43)

8) The Bodily, Visible Return of Christ (Rev 1:7; Jn 14:1-3; Mt 24:
    29-31; Rev 19:11-16)

9) The Substitutionary Death of Christ (1 Pt 2:24; 3:18; 2 Cor 5:21;
    1 Cor 5:7; Jn 1:29; Mt 1:21; 2 Cor 5:15)

Course: Christian World View (11th grade Bible)
Instructor: Dr. Fernandes

The Doctrine of God

1) <u>God's Existence</u>
    A) <u>God has revealed His existence through nature</u>
        1) this is called natural revelation
        2) through creation (Romans 1:18-22; Psalm 19:1)
        3) through conscience (Romans 2:14-15)
    B) <u>arguments for God's existence</u>
        1) universe had a beginning & needs a Cause
        2) design & order in universe imply an intelligent Designer
        3) eternal, unchanging moral laws imply an eternal, unchanging moral Lawgiver
        4) the absurdity of life without God
    C) <u>God has revealed Himself through supernatural means (supernatural revelation)</u>
        1) miracles, prophecies, the Bible
        2) Jesus (the God-man)

2) <u>False Views of God</u>
    A) <u>Atheism</u>—denial of God's existence
    B) <u>Agnosticism</u>—we cannot know if God exists
    C) <u>Deism</u>—God is not involved with His creation
    D) <u>Pantheism</u>—God is the universe (impersonal god)
    E) <u>Polytheism</u>—the existence of many gods
    F) <u>Dualism</u>—two gods, one good & one evil

3) <u>The Biblical View of God</u>
    A) <u>God is spirit</u> (John 4:24)
    B) <u>God is personal</u> (Exodus 20:2; John 3:16)
    C) <u>there is only one God</u> (Deuteronomy 6:4; 1 Timothy 2:5; Isaiah 43:10; 45:5; 46:9)

D) <u>this one God is three Persons</u>
    1) Father is God (1 Peter 1:2; Galatians 1:1)
    2) Son is God (Titus 2:13; Isaiah 9:6; John 1:1, 14)
    3) Holy Spirit is God (Acts 5:3-4;
       1 Corinthians 3:16)
    4) they are three separate Persons
       (Matthew 3:16-17; Genesis 1:26-27;
       John 14:16-17, 26; 15:26)
E) <u>doctrine of the Trinity</u>—there is only one true God, but this one God eternally exists as three equal Persons.

4) <u>God's Attributes</u>
    A) good (Matthew 19:17)
    B) eternal (no beginning & no end; Psalm 90:2)
    C) omnipresent (everywhere present; Psalm 139:7-8)
    D) omnipotent (all-powerful; Matthew 19:25-26)
    E) omniscient (all-knowing; Psalm 147:5)
    F) immutable (never changes; Hebrews 13:8; 1:10-12)
    G) sovereign (always in control; Isaiah 46:9-11)
    H) holy (separated from evil, absolutely pure;
       1 Peter 1:14-16)
    I) righteous (His deeds are just; 2 Timothy 4:7-8)
    J) true (He cannot lie; 1 Samuel 15:29; John 14:6)
    K) faithful (absolutely loyal; 1 Thessalonians 5:24)
    L) merciful (spares us the punishment we deserve;
       Ephesians 2:4)
    M) gracious (gives us the salvation we don't deserve;
       Ephesians 2:8-9)
    N) loving (unconditional seeking of the highest good
       for others; John 3:16; 1 John 4:8)

5) <u>The Names of God</u>
    A) <u>Old Testament Hebrew Names of God</u>
        1) <u>Elohim</u> (mighty warrior; Genesis 1:1)
        2) <u>El</u> (God)
            a) El Elyon (strongest strong one; Isa 14:14)
            b) El Roi (strong one who sees; Gn 16:13)
            c) El Shaddai (almighty God; Psalm 91:1)
            d) El Olam (the everlasting God; Isa 40:28)
        3) <u>Adonai</u> (Master, Lord; Psalm 110:1)
        4) <u>Yahweh or Jehovah</u> (the self-existent God of the covenant; Exodus 3:14)
            a) Jehovah Jireh (the Lord who provides; Genesis 22:13-14)
            b) Jehovah Nissi (the Lord my banner; Exodus 17:10-16)
            c) Jehovah Shalom (the Lord my peace; Judges 6:22-24)
            d) Jehovah Sabbaoth (the Lord of Hosts; 1 Samuel 1:3)
            e) Jehovah M'Kaddesh (the Lord my sanctifier; Exodus 31:13)
            f) Jehovah Rohi (the Lord my shepherd; Psalm 23:1)
            g) Jehovah Tsidkenu (the Lord our righteousness; Jeremiah 23:5-6)
            h) Jehovah Shammah (the Lord who is present; Ezekiel 48:35)
            i) Jehovah Rapha (the Lord our healer; Exodus 15:26)
    B) <u>New Testament Greek Names of God</u>
        1) <u>Theos</u> (God; John 1:1)
        2) <u>Lord</u> (Kurios; Mark 12:30-31; Acts 10:36)

Christian World View

1) What practical differences are there if the Christian God exists rather than a deistic God?

2) What practical differences are there if the Christian God exists rather than a pantheistic God?

3) What practical differences are there if Christianity is true and atheism is false?

4) How do the names of God show that God is
personal?

5) How do the attributes of God show that God is
personal?

Bibliology

1) <u>What is the Bible?</u>
   a. God's Word written in man's language (2 Tm 3:16-17; 2 Pt 1:20-21)
   b. Our final authority for faith & practice (Rev 22:18-19; Prov 30:5-6; Eph 2:19-20)
   c. God revealing Himself & His salvation to lost mankind (Is 45:22; Jn 14:6)
2) <u>False views of the Bible</u>
   a. Liberal view – the Bible is a human book filled with error
   b. Neo-orthodoxy – Bible contains errors, but becomes God's Word to us as we encounter God during a moment of crisis
   c. Partial theory – Bible has historical & scientific errors, but speaks truth when it deals with religious & moral issues
3) <u>Revelation</u> – God makes Himself & His Truth known to us
4) <u>Inspiration</u> – God guided human authors to record His Word without error
   a. <u>inerrancy</u>– Bible is totally without errors.
5) <u>Illumination</u> – holy Spirit enlightens our minds to receive truths from God's word
6) <u>The canon</u> – the list of books that belong in the Bible
7) <u>Original languages</u>
   a. Old Testament – primarily Hebrew
   b. New Testament – Koine or Common Greek

8) <u>Why God wrote the Bible</u>
   a. To reveal His salvation to lost mankind
   b. To reveal to believers how we should live

9) <u>Bible overview</u>
   a. Books of the Bible
   b. Overview of Bible History

Canonization

1) <u>revelation</u> (God made known His Word to the biblical authors; not dictation)

2) <u>inspiration</u> (God guided human authors to record His Word without errors)

3) <u>inerrancy</u> (the Bible is totally without errors in the original manuscripts)

4) <u>illumination</u> (the Holy Spirit enlightens our hearts & minds to understand His Word)

5) <u>canonization</u> (the Holy Spirit guided the church to properly identify which books belong in the Bible)

6) <u>preservation</u> (God sees to it that accurate copies of His Word will be preserved throughout the centuries)

Tests for Canonization

1) Apostolic authorship or authority
   (authoritative eyewitnesses & pupils of
   Jesus' ministry)

2) edifying (profitable) for the entire church

3) in agreement with previous revelation

The DaVinci Code

1)Dan Brown's novel; Ron Howard's movie
2)Brown claims that true history is a lie & that his conspiracy theory of the
    history of Christianity is true (*Holy Blood, Holy Grail*)
3)Jesus was married to Mary Magdalene—why was she named after her
    town?
4)when Jesus died, Mary Magdalene was pregnant with Jesus' daughter
5)Jesus never claimed to be God
6)He wanted Mary Magdalene to lead His church after His death
7)Peter & the Apostles objected—Mary Magdalene had to flee to France &
    remain in hiding
8)her descendants inter-married with the secret French royal line
9)Knights Templar & other secret societies protected the secret line of Jesus
10)Leonardo DaVinci was part of a secret society that guarded the secrets of
    Jesus' royal line (the Last Supper, the Sacred Feminine)
11)At the Council of Nicea in 325 ad, Emperor Constantine forced the
    bishops to vote to make Jesus God (before that, He was considered
    merely a man) {actually, homoousios vs homoiousios}

30 ad	50 ad	100 ad	325 ad
Creeds	Paul's	Jesus Seminar	DaVinci Code
Hymns	letters		
Sermons			
Larry Hurtado			
Galatians 1 & 2			

12)Constantine ordered the burning of the "true" Gospels & ordered the
    canonization of the New Testament books we have today (the New
    Testament does not represent original Christianity)
13)Gnostics believed Jesus was merely a man (actually, they were docetists)
14)Matthew, Mark, Luke, & John deny Jesus' humanity (hypostatic union)
15)original Christianity was a sex cult involved in secret rituals & goddess
    worship
16)Tests for canonization (apostolic authorship or authority, edifying for the
    entire church, doesn't contradict previous scriptures)
17)Gnostic writings written after 140 ad, rejected Old Testament, heretical

The Gospel of Judas

1)Irenaeus warned Christians about *The Gospel of Judas* in 180 ad
2)recently, a Coptic copy of the Greek original was found and translated
3)the copy dates to about 300 ad, while the original was probably written
     between 160 and 180 ad
4)*The Gospel of Judas* confirms what Irenaeus said about it:
     A)it is a Gnostic document
     B)docetism—Jesus only appeared to be a man
     C)flesh = totally evil; spirit = good
     D)read excerpts from *The Gospel of Judas*
     E)salvation through secret knowledge (gnosis)
     F)*The Gospel of Judas* is a Cainite Gnostic writing
     G)Gnostic teachings not taught by the Apostles
5)overview of *The Gospel of Judas*
     A)Jesus is a Gnostic teacher of Divine wisdom & mysteries; Jesus
       often appeared to the disciples as a child?
     B)Judas is His greatest disciple; only he could understand the higher
       spiritual knowledge (the gnosis)
     C)other 11 apostles served the evil OT Creator God who indwelt them
     D)Jesus expressed the divinity of the true God
     E)Jesus asks Judas to betray Him so Jesus could rid Himself of His
       body (He asks Judas to "sacrifice the man that clothes me")
     F)each person has his own star—Judas' star is greater than the other
       Apostles
     G)Sethians = the Gnostics (the divine race) came from Seth (the
       Christ); Barbelo = the divine mother of all (1 Jn 2:22-23)
     H)the traditional Christian Church is evil & will be judged
     I)Jesus is a divine spark that needs to be set free from His body
     J)Judas will be cursed by the apostles, but will someday rule over
       them
     K)complex Gnostic cosmology dealing with aeons
     L)Sophia = the symbol for divine wisdom
     M)Judas is glorified & transfigured much like Jesus in the Gospels
     N)Jesus' death & resurrection are not really important
6)test for canonization—apostolic authorship or authority, spiritually
     edifying for the entire church, consistent with previous revelation of
     Old & New Testaments (discuss evidence for NT books)
7)Gnostic writings—written too late & contradicted Old Testament &
     Apostolic teachings

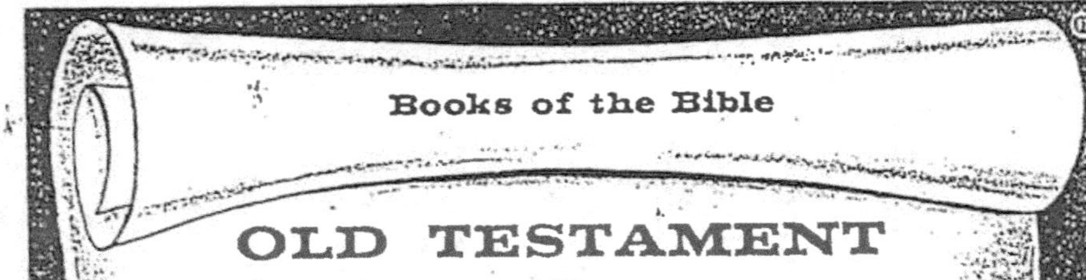

Books of the Bible

OLD TESTAMENT

39

HISTORY

THE PENTATEUCH (Books of Moses or of the Law) (5)

Genesis	Leviticus	Deuteronomy
Exodus	Numbers	

THE HISTORICAL BOOKS (12)

Joshua	Second Samuel	Second Chronicles
Judges	First Kings	Ezra
Ruth	Second Kings	Nehemiah
First Samuel	First Chronicles	Esther

POETRY

THE POETICAL and WISDOM BOOKS (5)

Job	Proverbs	Song of Solomon
Psalms	Ecclesiastes	

PROPHECY

THE MAJOR PROPHETS (5)

Isaiah	Lamentations	Daniel
Jeremiah	Ezekiel	

THE MINOR PROPHETS (12)

Hosea	Obadiah	Nahum	Haggai
Joel	Jonah	Habakkuk	Zechariah
Amos	Micah	Zephaniah	Malachi

Books of the Bible

NEW TESTAMENT

27

HISTORY

THE GOSPELS (4)

Matthew	Luke
Mark	John

THE BOOK of ACTS (1)

EPISTLES

THE PAULINE EPISTLES (13)

Romans	Colossians
First Corinthians	First Thessalonians
Second Corinthians	Second Thessalonians
Galatians	First Timothy
Ephesians	Second Timothy
Philippians	Titus
Philemon	

THE GENERAL EPISTLES (8)

Hebrews	First John
James	Second John
First Peter	Third John
Second Peter	Jude

PROPHECY

THE BOOK of REVELATION (1)

Historical Overview of the Bible

1) <u>Creation Period</u> (ancient history of human race)
   a. Creation, fall, flood, tower
   b. Genesis 1-11
2) <u>Patriarch period</u> (start of Jewish nation)
   a. Abraham
   b. Isaac
   c. Jacob (Genesis 12-50)
   d. Joseph & 11 brothers (12 tribes)
   e. Job
3) <u>Exodus period</u> (Moses delivers Israel out of Egypt)
   a. Exodus, Leviticus; Numbers, Deuteronomy
   b. Wilderness wandering
   c. 10 plagues, parting Red Sea
   d. Release from bondage in Egypt
4) <u>Conquest period</u> (Joshua & taking the Promised Land)
5) <u>Judges period</u> (13 judges of Israel; moral anarchy)
   a. Samson, Gideon, Jepthah
6) <u>United Kingdom period</u>
   a. Saul, David & Solomon
   b. Israel's glorious years
7) <u>Divided Kingdom period</u>
   a. 10 northern tribes (Israel) split with the 2 southern tribes (Judah) 900BC
   b. Northern tribes taken captive by Assyria (722 BC)

8) Captivity period (2 southern tribes under Babylonian rule)
- 605 – 538 BC
- 2 southern tribes under Babylonian rule
- 586 BC Temple destroyed

9) Return period (Medo-Persian rule)
- 12 tribes under Medo-Persian rule
- Jews allowed to return to the Holy Land
- Rebuilding temple & walls of Jerusalem
- 538 – 400 BC

10) 400 Silent years (no books written)
- Gap between Old & New testaments
- Jews under Greek rule, later Roman rule
- 400 – 5 BC

11) Gospel period (life of Jesus the Jewish Messiah)
- Under Roman rule
- Matthew, Mark, Luke, John
- 5 BC – 30 AD

12) Early Church period (Gospel spreads all over the world)
- Peter & Paul (Book of Acts)
- 30 AD- 60 AD

13) The Epistles (apostolic letters teaching Christians how to live Godly lives)
- 45 AD –100 AD

Christology
The Doctrine of Christ

1) His pre-existence – He existed before He became a man
2) His deity (see handout) Jesus is God the Son
3) Old Testament prophecies (see handout)
4) The incarnation – God the Son became a man
    a. The Kenosis (Php 2:5-11)
        i. God the Son humbled Himself by becoming a man
    b. The Hypostatic Union (John 1:1-18)
        i. Jesus is one Person with 2 natures forever (fully God & fully man)
5) Christ's earthly ministry
    a. His sinlessness – Jesus was conceived without a sin nature & lived totally without sin
    b. His miracles – Jesus performed miracles that confirmed the truth of His teachings
    c. His teachings – His deity, salvation through Him alone, the Kingdom of God (Pm 14:17; Rev 11:15; Mt 13)
    d. Opposition – Jewish religious leaders opposed Him
6) Christ's death & burial (1 Pt 2:24; 3:18)
    a. He died as a substitute sacrifice for us
    b. He took out punishment for us & died in out place
    c. He paid the penalty for our sins

<u>Christology (2)</u>

7) Christ's resurrection

- Jesus bodily rose from the dead (Jn 2; Lk 24; Jn 20)

- Jesus conquered death for us

- Jesus appeared alive to His disciples for a period of 40 days

8) Christ's ascension – Jesus retuned to Heaven & is seated at the Father's right hand

9) Christ's present ministry – he intercedes for us & protects us (1 Jn 2:1-2)

10) Christ's return – Jesus will visibly return to earth (Mt 24:29-31)

11) Christ's millennial reign (Rev 20)

- Jesus will reign on earth for 1,000 years

INSTITUTE OF BIBLICAL DEFENSE
*P. O. Box 3264, Bremerton, WA. 98310 * (360) 698-7382*
Dr. Phil Fernandes, President

THE DEITY OF CHRIST

1) The Apostles Called Jesus God
   A) John (John 1:1, 14; 1 John 5:20)
   B) Peter (2 Peter 1:1)
   C) Paul (Romans 9:5; Philippians 2:5-8;
      Colossians 2:9; Titus 2:13; Acts 20:28)
   D) Thomas (John 20:26-29)
   E) Matthew (Matthew 1:20-23)

2) The Old Testament Prophets Called Jesus God
   A) Isaiah (Isaiah 7:14; 9:6)
   B) Micah (Micah 5:2)
   C) Zechariah (Zechariah 14:5)
   D) Jeremiah (Jeremiah 23:5-6)

3) God the Father Called Jesus God (Hebrews 1:8)

4) Jesus Called Himself God (John 5:17-18; 22-23; 8:23-24,
      58-59; Exodus 3:13-14; John 10:30-33; 14:9; 17:5;
      Revelation 1:8, 17-18; 22:12-13; Isaiah 44:6)

5) Jesus Acted as if He is God
   A) He accepted worship (Exodus 20:1-6; Matthew
      2:11; 14:33; 28:9; John 9:35-38; 20:26-29)
   B) He forgave sins (Mark 2:5-7)
   C) He was arrested for blasphemy (Mark 14:64;
      John 10:33)
   D) He created the universe (John 1:1-3; Colossians
      1:15-17; Genesis 1:1)
   E) Jesus is called the Lord (kurios - Greek word for
      Hebrew word YHWH) John 20:28; Acts 10:36
   F) Every knee will bow to Jesus (Philippians 2:9-11;
      Isaiah 45:22-23)

Old Testament Prophecies Fulfilled By Christ

<u>Old Testament Prophecy</u>   <u>New Testament Fulfillment</u>

1) seed of Abraham (Genesis 12:1-3)________________________
2) tribe of Judah (Genesis 49:10)________________________
3) line of Jesse (Isaiah 11:1) ________________________
4) line of David (Jeremiah 23:5) ________________________
5) virgin birth (Isaiah 7:14)________________________
6) born in Bethlehem (Micah 5:2)________________________
7) His forerunner (Isaiah 40:3)________________________
8) executed before 70AD (Daniel 9:24-27)________________________
9) His miracles (Isaiah 35:4-6)________________________
10) His parables (Psalm 78:2)________________________
11) rejected by the Jews (Isaiah 53; 65:1-2; 8:13-15)

____

12) wide Gentile following (Isaiah 42:1-4; 65:1-2)

____

13) betrayed for 30 pieces of silver (Zechariah 11:12-13)

____

14) forsaken by His disciples (Zechariah 13:7)________________
15) entered Jerusalem on a donkey, received a King's welcome
        (Zechariah 9:9)________________________
16) silent before His accusers (Isaiah 53:7)________________________
17) crucified (Psalm 22:16)________________________
18) lots cast for His garments (Psalm 22:18)________________________
19) bones not broken (Psalm 34:20; Exodus 12:43-46)

____

20) side pierced (Zechariah 12:10)________________________
21) buried in a rich man's tomb (Isaiah 53:9)________________
22) resurrection (Psalm 16:10)________________________
23) ascension (Psalm 68:18)________________________
24) at the Father's right hand (Psalm 110:1)________________________

<u>John 1:1-18</u>

1. Jesus is eternal (vs. 1,2)

2. Jesus is God (vs. 1,2)

3. Jesus is creator (vs. 3)

4. In Jesus is life (vs. 4)

5. Jesus gives light (vs. 4-5)

    a. Spiritual enlightenment

    b. Spiritual purity

6. Jesus is the true light (vs. 9)

7. Jesus enlightens every man (vs. 9)

8. Jesus came into the world (vs. 9)

9. The world did not recognize Jesus, the creator (vs. 10)

10. His people, the Jews, rejected Jesus (vs. 11)

11. Jesus gives those who believe in Him the right to become Children of God (vs. 12)

12. Believers are born of God (vs. 13)

13. Jesus became a man (vs. 14)

14. Jesus is full of grace & truth (vs. 14)

15. Jesus perfectly reveals God to man (vs. 18)

<u>Philippians 2:5-11</u>

Vs. 5) Have the same attitude as Jesus

Vs. 6) Jesus is God, but didn't cling to his privileges as God

Vs. 7) Jesus humbled himself by becoming a man

Vs. 8) Jesus humbled himself to the point of death on a cross

Vs. 9) God the Father exalted Jesus to the supreme position

Vs. 10) every knee will bow before Jesus

Vs. 11) everyone will acknowledge that Jesus is Lord

Jesus' Teachings

6 Themes

1) <u>The Kingdom of God</u> (Mt 13)

    a. Wherever God rules

    b. Present/spiritual stage – in believer's hearts

    c. Future/physical stage – when Christ reigns on Earth

2) <u>He is God</u> (Jn 5:17-18; 8:23-24, 58-59; 10:30; 17:5; 14:9)

3) <u>He is Savior</u> (Jn 3:16-18; 14:6)

4) <u>He is Messiah</u> (The one God anointed to rescue Israel) Mt 16; Jn 4; Mk 14

5) <u>True Spirituality</u> (Mt 5, 6, 7 – Sermon on the Mount)

6) <u>He will return</u> (Mt 24)

<u>Doctrine of Salvation – Memorization Verses</u>

<u>Romans 3:23</u> – "For all have sinned and fall short of the glory of God"

<u>Romans 5:8</u> – "But God demonstrates His own love for us, in that Christ died for us while we were yet sinners"

<u>Romans 6:23</u> – "For the wages of sin is death, but the free gift of God is eternal life through Christ Jesus our Lord"

<u>John 3:16</u> – "For God so loved the world that he gave His only begotten Son that whosoever believes in Him shall not perish but have eternal life"

<u>John 14:6</u> – Jesus said to Him, "I am the Way, the Truth, and the Life. No one comes to the Father except through me."

<u>John 11:25-26</u> – Jesus said to her, "I am the Resurrection and the Life; He who believes in me will live even if he dies. And everyone who lives and believes in me will never die."

<u>Ephesians 2:8-9</u> – For by grace you have been saved through faith and that not of yourselves it is the gift of God not as a result of works, that no one should boast."

Soteriology – Vocabulary Words

Salvation – the act of delivering someone out of danger

Redemption – the setting free of someone by the paying
of a price

Forgiveness – the canceling of someone's debt

Propitiation – satisfaction

Substitute sacrifice – Jesus died in our place and took
out punishment for us

Grace

- Unmerited favor

- Receiving the salvation we don't deserve

Mercy – the sparing of judgment that we do deserve

Faith – the act of trusting in or relying upon

Justification – when God declares a sinner righteous at
the moment he first believes

Sanctification -- the process through which we
progressively become more set apart for God's holy
purposes

Glorification – when God finishes the work He starts in a
believer; when God perfects us

Imputation – to credit something to another person's
account

Romans 3:10-31

1) There is none righteous

2) No one seeks God

3) No one does good

4) No one is declared righteous in God's sight by obeying

   the law

5) The law makes us conscious of our sin

6) Righteousness comes through faith in Jesus

7) All have sinned & fall short of the glory of God

8) Believers are justified freely by God's grace

9) Through redemption in Jesus

10)   Jesus was sacrificed for us

11)   God remains just

12)   God justifies those who trust in Jesus

13)   We have no reason to boast

14)   We are justified by faith apart from the law

15)   God justifies both Jew & Gentile by faith

16)   Once saved, we uphold the law by faith

Ephesians 2:8-10

1) Saved by grace alone

2) Through faith alone

3) In Jesus alone

4) Salvation is a gift of God

5) Not a result of works

6) We have no reasons to boast

7) Believers are God's work of art

8) We are new Christians – created to do good works

9) Christians don't do good works to get saved

10) Christians do good work because we are saved

11) Good works are not the cause (or root) of salvation

12) Good works are the result (or fruit) of salvation

<u>John 14:6 & Acts 4:12</u>

Salvation comes only through Jesus

<u>John 3:16-18</u>

1) God loves the world

2) God sent His Son

3) Whoever believes in God's son is saved

4) God sent His son to save, not to condemn

5) Whoever rejects God's son remains condemned

<u>1 John 2:23; Luke 10:16; Matthew 10:32-33</u>

1) Those who reject the son reject the Father

2) Those who accept the Son accept the Father

3) True believers publicly acknowledge Jesus

<u>1 Peter 2:24; 3:18</u>

<u>2 Corinthians 5:15, 21; John 1:29;</u>

<u>1 Corinthians 5:7</u>

1)Jesus died on the cross for our sins

2)He took our punishment for us

3)He was sacrificed for us

4)He took our sins; we receive His

 righteousness

5)The just one died for the unjust

The Salvation Message

1) We are sinners; we cannot save ourselves (Rm 3:23; Mt 19:25)

2) Jesus is the only way for us to be saved (Jn 14:6)

3) Jesus died on the cross for our sins (1 Pt 2:24; 3:18; Jn 1:29)

4) Jesus rose from the dead to conquer death for us (1 Cor 15:3-8; 14, 17, 54-57)

5) We must trust in Jesus alone for salvation (Jn 3:16-18; 11:25-26)

The Logic of Salvation

1) <u>God loves us</u>
   a. He doesn't force His love on us
   b. He gave us the freedom to accept or reject His love
   c. We rejected God's love & rebelled against Him

2) <u>God is totally just</u>
   a. He must judge & punish all sin
   b. He cannot have fellowship with sin
   c. He cannot forgive sin unless it's paid for in full
   d. All sin is rebellion against God
   e. All sin earns the ultimate punishment (hell – eternal separation from God)
   f. Any substitute sacrifice must be ultimately worthy
   g. Any substitute sacrifice must be able to die

3) <u>God loves us</u>
   a. He sent His ultimately worthy Son to become a man (our substitute sacrifice)
   b. He punished His son in our place
   c. He will not force His love & forgiveness on us
   d. We have the freedom to accept or reject God's love and forgiveness by accepting or rejecting Jesus as Savior

4) <u>God is all powerful</u>
   a. He conquered death for us by raising Jesus from the dead
   b. Jesus' resurrection guarantees the resurrection to life of all believers

5) <u>The substitute sacrifice had to be God</u>
   a. For it had to be ultimately worthy

6) <u>The substitute sacrifice had to be a man</u>
   a. For He had to represent man
   b. For He had to be able to die for our sins

Predestination & Free Will

Calvinism	Arminianism
T – Total Depravity	- Prevenient Grace
U – Unconditional Election	- Conditional election
L – Limited atonement	- Unlimited atonement
I – Irresistible grace	- Resistible grace
P – Perseverance of the Saints	- Believer can lose their salvation

Reconciling Divine Sovereignty & Free Will

1) <u>Hyper-Calvinism</u> – humans have no free will at all; everything is predetermined
2) <u>Calvinism</u>
   a. Regeneration precedes faith
   b. We aren't free to accept Jesus
   c. God must first give us a new nature
3) <u>Arminianism</u>
   a. Faith precedes regeneration
   b. We are free to accept Jesus
   c. God gives believers a new nature
4) <u>Radical Arminianism</u> – God cannot infallibly foreknow human future free choices
5) <u>My view</u> (a type of Molinism)
   a. God actualizes the greatest possible world (the world in which the greatest number are saved)
   b. God predestines (predetermines) to bring about those circumstances that would persuade potential believers to freely accept Jesus

Hyper Calvinism—no free will at all

Calvinism—regeneration precedes faith, monergism

Arminianism—faith precedes regeneration, synergism

Semi-Pelagianism—salvation by faith plus works

Pelagianism—salvation by works; follow Jesus' example

Open Theism—God does not infallibly foreknow future
free choices

Religious Pluralism—all religions lead to God

Inclusivism—good people are included in Christ's
salvation even if they don't believe

Universalism—everyone is or will be saved

Exclusivism—salvation only through faith in Jesus

<u>Anthropology (doctrine of man)</u>
1)Origin – created by God in God's image
2)Identity – Fallen; inherited a sin nature
3)Destination – heaven or hell (depending on
   one's response to Jesus)
4)Composition – body & soul

<u>Hamartiology (doctrine of sin)</u>
1)The Fall – Adam & Eve sinned in the garden
2)Inherited sin nature – we inherit a sin nature
   from them
3)Cannot save ourselves – we deserve hell &
   can't earn our way to heaven

<u>Angelology (doctrine of angels)</u>
  1)Created directly by God
  2)Spirit beings /no bodies
  3)Serve God & minist4er to man
  4)Will eventually spend eternity in Heaven

<u>Satanology (doctrine of Satan)</u>
  1)The highest fallen angel
  2)Wanted to be like God & rebelled against
    him
  3)Leads the fallen angels (demons)
  4)Will eventually spend eternity in hell
  5)Opposes God

<u>Demonology (doctrine of demons)</u>
  1)Fallen angels
  2)Unclean spirits
  3)Possess people
  4)Tempt people
  5)Follow Satan
  6)Will eventually spend eternity in hell
  7) Oppose God

Ekklesia – a called out assembly

<u>Ecclesiology</u> (doctrine of the church)

1) <u>Universal church</u> – all true believers
2) <u>Local churches</u> – local assembly of believers
3) <u>Church government</u> (different views)
   a. <u>Monarchial</u> – Pope rules (Roman Catholic)
   b. <u>Episcopal</u> – Bishops rule (Episcopal, Anglican)
   c. <u>Presbyterian</u> – elders rule
   d. <u>Congregational</u> – congregation rules (Baptist)
4) <u>Church ordinances</u>
   a. Lord's supper
   b. Water baptism

<u>Eschatology (End-Times)</u>
1) <u>Premillennialism</u> – Christ returns before the millennium & literally reigns on Earth for 1,000 yrs.)
2) <u>Amillennialism</u> – no millennium on Earth; Jesus reigns from Heaven
3) <u>Postmillennialism</u> – Christ returns after the Church reigns on Earth for a long period of time
4) <u>Pretribulationalism</u> – Christ secretly snatches the Church away before the 7 year period of Tribulation
5) <u>Midtribulationalism</u> – Christ secretly snatches the Church away in the middle of the Tribulation
6) <u>Posttribulationalism</u> – Christ returns after the tribulation for the Church; rapture = 2nd coming
7) <u>Antichrist</u> – Demon-possessed man who will rule the world in the last days
8) <u>False prophet</u> – right-hand man of the antichrist also demon-possessed
9) <u>Mark of the Beast</u> – mark on right hand or forehead; needed to buy or sell in Antichrist's reign (666)

- Rev 19:11-21; Rev 20; 2 Thes 2;
- Rev 13; Mt 24:1-31

Christian World View

Part 2

<u>Apologetics</u>

*The Defense of
the Christian Faith*

<u>Evidence for God's Existence</u>

1) <u>Cosmological argument</u> – the universe had a beginning and needs a cause

2) <u>Continuing existence of the universe</u> – the existence of dependent beings necessitates the existence of a totally independent Being

3) <u>Teleological argument</u> – the design in the universe needs an intelligent Designer

4) <u>Possibility of human knowledge (human reason)</u> – human reason needs a rational cause

5) <u>Existence of universal, eternal, unchanging truths</u> – their source is an eternal, unchanging Mind

6) <u>Universal, eternal, unchanging moral laws</u> – prove the existence of an eternal, unchanging Moral Lawgiver

7) <u>The meaning of life (purpose)</u> – if God does not exist, life is absurd

8) <u>Reason to be optimistic about the future (hope)</u> – God & eternal life are needed for eternal hope

9) <u>Guarantee that evil will be defeated</u> – apart from the death, resurrection & return of Jesus there is no guarantee that evil will be defeated

10)   <u>Feelings of guilt</u> – deep down inside we all know we have sinned against a Holy God

11) <u>Fear of death</u> – animals fear pain of dying, but humans fear what comes after death

12) <u>Respect for human life (human rights)</u> – in universe without God, there are no human rights

13) <u>Free will & human responsibility</u> – if only matter exists, then there is no such thing as free will & we are not responsible for our actions

14) <u>Pascal's Wager</u>

Pascal's Wager

	God exists	God does not exist
Wager against God	Lose everything (infinite loss)	Win nothing
Wager for God	Win everything (infinite gain)	Lose nothing

<u>The Case for Creation</u>
<u>(Norman Geisler & J, Kirby Anderson)</u>

1)<u>the origin of the universe</u>—the universe had a beginning & needs a cause (2nd law of thermodynamics, big bang)

2)<u>the origin of life</u>—intelligent intervention is needed (single celled animal contains enough genetic information to fill 1,000 complete sets of Encyclopedia Britannica)

3)<u>the origin of more complex life forms</u>—the human brain contains enough information to fill 20 million volumes of encyclopedia

*In each case the creation model is more scientifically plausible than the evolution model

The Case against Evolution

The evolutionary model has many unproven assumptions:

1)the universe popped into existence totally out of nothing totally without a cause

2)a random explosion (the big bang) produced all the order, design, & complexity we see in the universe today

3)life evolved from non-life without intelligent intervention

4)multi-celled animals evolved from single-celled animals without intelligent intervention

5)animals with backbones came from animals without backbones

6)the common ancestry of fish, reptiles, birds, & mammals (common anatomy could point to common design)

*Therefore, evolution itself is an unproven assumption

Creation vs. Evolution

Problems with Evolution

1) Modern science was founded by Christians
2) Beginning of the universe (big bang, 2nd law of thermodynamics)
3) First life (DNA, specified complexity)
4) Complex life forms (human brain, fossil record)
5) No transitional forms (fossil record, reptiles to birds, apes to humans, fish gills to lungs)
6) Many unproven assumptions of evolution
   a. Eternal universe or universe popped into existence from nothing without a cause
   b. Life from non-life (without intelligent intervention)
   c. Intelligence from non-intelligence
   d. Multi-celled animals from single-celled animals
   e. Vertebrate from invertebrate
   f. Common ancestry of fish, reptiles, birds, & mammals

Refuting Moral Relativism

1) Moral relativism – each individual decides for themselves what is right & what is wrong

2) Moral absolutes – same moral laws apply to all people at all times in all places.

3) Argument for absolute moral law

    a. Moral law doesn't ultimately originate with the individual, for then we could not condemn the actions of another person (Hitler)

    b. Moral law is not the creation of each society, for then one society could not condemn the actions of another society (Nazi Germany)

    c. Moral lay doesn't come from a world consensus
        i. Not infallible (flat world, geocentric universe, slavery, women's rights)
        ii. Even atheists try to change the world for the better

    d. A moral law qualitatively above all men
        i. Not descriptive of the way things are.
        ii. It is prescriptive of the way things ought to be (Prescriber needed)
        iii. We need a moral lawgiver qualitatively above all mankind
        iv. If we wish to condemn the actions of the past, this moral lawgiver must also be eternal & unchanging

The Problem of Evil & Human Suffering

The Origin of Evil

1)God created everything that exists.

2)Evil is something that exists.

3)Therefore, God created evil.

Christian Response:

1)God created everything that exists *in itself.*

2)Evil is something that exists in something good.

3)Therefore, evil is a corruption or a perversion of something that was originally created good.

4)Hence, God created the possibility for evil (free will), not evil itself.

5)We actualized the possibility of evil by disobeying God.

6)Evil is a privation (a lack of a good that should be there).

The Continuing Existence of Evil

1)An all-good God would not want evil to exist.

2)All-powerful God is able to prevent evil from existing.

3)But, evil exists.

4)Therefore, no all-good, all-powerful God exists.

Christian Response:

1)An all-good God would not want evil to exist *except for
the purposes of a greater good.*

2)An all-powerful God is able to prevent evil from existing.

3)But, evil exists.

4)Therefore, God allows evil to exist for purposes of a
greater good.

Evil & Human Suffering

1) God created the possibility of evil (free will), not evil itself
2) Evil is a privation (a lack of a good that should be there)
3) God's love cannot be forced on His creatures
4) God allows evil for the purpose of a greater good (free will)
5) Unnecessary time limit placed on God (God is in the process of defeating evil)
6) Man's free choice brought evil & human suffering into the world
7) God will use evil for good purposes (love enemies, forgive, courage, etc)
8) God's ways & thoughts are far above ours (Is. 55:8-9)
9) This is not the greatest possible world (this is the greatest possible way to achieve the greatest possible world – heaven)
10) Atheists usually deny the existence of evil
11) God will defeat evil through Christ's death, resurrection, return
12) The God of the Bible is the only guarantee that evil will ultimately be defeated
13) Many people turn to God during times of suffering
14) God often uses suffering to test us and help us to grow

Old Testament Reliability

1) Archaeological digs – primary evidence for Old Testament

2) Manuscript evidence

    a. Masoretic Text – standard Hebrew test (900 AD)

    b. Dead Sea Scrolls – Hebrew OT manuscripts found in Dead Sea/Qumran area (150 AD)

    c. Septuagint – Greek translation of Hebrew OT (200 BC)

New Testament Reliability

<u>Manuscript evidence</u> -- New Testament – most reliable of all ancient writings

- More copies (NT – 26,000 / Homer's Iliad – 643 / Plato – 7)
- Wider distribution
- Smallest gap between earliest copy & original (NT – 25 yrs., HI – 500 yrs., PL – 1,200)
- Accuracy – agreement between copies (NT – 99.5%, HI – 95%)

<u>Apostolic Fathers</u> – pupils of the apostles whom the apostles appointed to lead the early church.
- Quoted NT, taught Christ's deity, sacrificial death, resurrection, and salvation through Jesus alone.
- Clement of Rome (95 AD)
- Ignatius (115 AD)
- Polycarp (died 156 AD)
- Papias (60-140 AD) (Recorded by Ireneaus – 180 AD)

<u>Ancient Secular Writings</u> – confirmed message of early church
- Thallus
- Tacitus
- Pliny the younger
- Emperor Trajan
- Emperor Hadrian
- Suetonius
- Josephus
- Jewish Talmud
- Lucian

Ancient Creeds in New Testament
- Paul's writing (50's & 60's AD)
- Romans 10:9 (Deity and resurrection)
- 1 Cor. 15:3-8 (resurrection)
- Php 2:6-11 (Christ's deity)

NT Reliability (2)

Confirmation by experts
- A.T. Robinson
- Sir William Ramsay
- William F. Albright
- Sir Frederick Kenyon
- Millar Burrows
- F.F. Bruce
- Bruce Metzger

Additional Evidences

1) Matthew – testimony of Papias – originally written in Hebrew, tax collection – stenographer, quoted very early
2) Mark – testimony of Papias, Peter's Gospel, quoted early
3) Luke & Acts – Acts was Luke's sequel, both addressed to Theopilus, Paul's death not recorded, quoted early
4) John – quoted or paraphrased by Ignatius, Polycarp,
   a. Papias attests to John's authorship
5) Paul's letters – except general epistles, widely accepted (50's & 60's AD)
6) Hebrews – before 70 AD, temple sacrifices still offered

Tests for Canonization

1) Apostolic authorship or authority
   (authoritative eyewitnesses & pupils of
   Jesus' ministry)

2) edifying (profitable) for the entire church

3) in agreement with previous revelation

Miracles

1) Definition – a miracle is an act of God interrupting the ordinary causes of events
2) David Hume & Benedict Spinoza
   a. Miracles violate natural laws
   b. No reasonable person would accept an exception to natural laws
3) Natural laws – descriptive, not prescriptive (they describe the way things generally occur; they don't prescribe what can or cannot occur)
4) God is above the laws of nature, He can supercede or interrupt them as He chooses
5) Once someone accepts the existence of the God of the Bible, miracle are possible
6) Biblical miracles confirm faith in the true God & authenticate the message & messenger or alleviate suffering
7) Miracles are not performed to entertain
8) Reliable eyewitness testimony confirms the reality of Jesus' miracles (martyrs' deaths)
9) Pagan miracles
   a. Lack eyewitness testimony
   b. Some contradict their own religion (Hinduism)
   c. Usually based on mythology or legends
   d. Demonic counterfeit
10) 3 periods of frequent miracles
   i. The Exodus (Moses)
   ii. The prophets of Israel (Elijah, Elisha)
   iii. Time of Christ & early church

<u>Christ's Resurrection (bodily resurrection)</u>

1) <u>Historical accounts</u>
      a. Matthew, Mark, Luke, John, Peter, Paul, apostolic fathers, Josephus
2) <u>Evidences for the resurrection</u>
      a. Peter's changed life
      b. Paul's changed life
      c. James's changed life
      d. Empty tomb
      e. Sabbath changed
      f. Appearances
      g. Reliable eyewitness testimony
      h. Martyr's death
      i. Lady witnesses
      j. Shroud
      k. Manuscript evidence
      l. Ancient creeds
      m. Apostolic fathers
      n. Ancient secular writings
3) <u>The meaning of the resurrection</u>
      a. Conquered death
      b. First fruits (guarantee of the resurrection of all believers)
      c. Confirmed His teachings
4) <u>Summary of Christ's post-resurrection appearances (1 Cor 15:3-8; Matt 28; Luke 24)</u>
      a. Peter
      b. 12 apostles
      c. Over 500
      d. James
      e. Apostles
      f. Paul
      g. Ladies
      h. 2 disciples on road to Emmaus
5) <u>Christ's resurrection was bodily (John 2; 20; Luke 24)</u>

Evidence for Jesus' Resurrection

<u>Are miracles possible?</u> -- Yes, if God exists.

<u>Christ's resurrection was bodily</u> – John 2; 20. Luke 24.

<u>Importance of the Resurrection</u> – No resurrection, no hope, no defeat of death
    (1 Cor 15:14, 17)

<u>Only 4 possibilities</u> – legends, lies, deceived, truth

<u>Resurrection accounts were not legends</u>
- NT reliability
  o Manuscript evidence
  o Ancient creeds
  o Apostolic fathers
  o Secular writings

<u>Apostles were not lying</u>
- Honest men
- Died martyr's deaths (sincere)

<u>Apostles were not deceived</u>
- Hallucinations happen in the mind
- 2 or more people can't have the same one

<u>Apostles were telling the truth</u>
- Wrong tomb theory
- Stolen body theory
- Swoon theory

<u>Further support for the resurrection</u>

1) Peter's changed life
2) Paul's changed life
3) James' changed life
4) Empty tomb
5) Woman – first witnesses
6) Worship day changed to Sunday
7) Church grew rapidly in Jerusalem
8) Shroud of Turin?
9) Post-resurrection appearances
10) Martyr's deaths (reliable witnesses)
11) Ancient creeds
12) Apostolic Fathers
13) Ancient secular writers
14) NT manuscript evidence
15) Failure of alternative theories
16) Apostles running away

Evidence for Christ's Deity

Jesus claimed to be God
- Called God his own father
- He said we should worship Him as we worship the Father
- I & the Father are one
- He called Himself the "I Am"
- Perfectly represents the Father
- He shared God's glory with Him before the world was
- Alpha & Omega, First & Last

The Apostles called Jesus God
- John
- Matthew
- Thomas
- Peter
- Paul

The Apostolic Fathers called Jesus God
- Clement of Rome
- Polycarp
- Ignatius

Ancient Secular Authors wrote that First-Century Christians Worshipped Jesus as God
- Pliny the Younger
- Lucian

Ancient Creeds call Jesus God
- Php 2:5-11
- 1 Tm 3:16
- Rm 10:9

<u>Evidence for Christ's Deity (2)</u>

<u>Only 3 choices: Liar, Insane, or God</u>

1) <u>Jesus was not a liar</u>
- He taught highest standards of morality ever taught
- Positive impact on mankind
- His love & compassion for others
- His resurrection (would God raise a liar)
- He wouldn't have died for a lie

2) <u>Jesus was not insane</u>
- Billions of followers
- Greatest teacher of all time (insane people make lousy teachers)
- His miraculous life
- His resurrection

3) <u>Conclusions – Jesus is God</u>
- The Old Testament prophecies He fulfilled
- Miracles
- Resurrection

Evidence the Bible is God's Word

A) Christ's teaching about the Old Testament
- a. Verses – Mt 5:17-18; 15:3-4; 22:31-32; Mk 7:9-13; Lk 11:44-51
- b. Jesus considered the OT the inerrant Word of God

B) Christ's teaching about the New Testament
- a. Verses – k 13:31; Jn 14:26; 5:26-27: 16:13; Acts 1:18
- b. Christ promised His teachings would be preserved
- c. The holy Spirit would remind apostles of Christ's words
- d. The Holy Spirit would show the apostles future things
- e. The Hoy Spirit would guide the apostles into the Truth
- f. The Holy Spirit would guide the apostles to be Christ's representation to the world
- g. Conclusions = Christ promised to preserve His teachings through the apostle's writings
- h. Jesus is God & He declared the Bible (both OT and NT) to be the inerrant Word of God

C) Further confirmation the Bible is God's Word
- i. Bible's supernatural wisdom
  - i. Explains man's greatness & wretchedness
  - ii. Solves problem of evil
  - iii. #1 all time best seller
  - iv. Most cherished wisdom

<u>Evidence the Bible is God's Word (2)</u>

      v. Scientific precision
          1. 700 BC – earth is sphere (Is. 40:22)
          2. 2000 BC – earth is suspended in space (Job 26:1)
          3. 1st & 2nd laws of thermodynamics (Gn 2:1-3; Mt 13:31)
   j. Fulfilled prophecies
     i. Cities (Tyre)
    ii. Nations (Egypt, Edom, Philistia)
  iii. Israel (captivity, scattered, regathering, continued existence)
   iv. Empires (Babylon, Medo-Persia, Greece, Rome)
     v. Messiah
D) Implications of the bible being God's Word – salvation, teachings, morality

World Views

1) <u>Atheism</u> – belief that there is no God
   a. Refutation
      i. No adequate explanation for the existence of the universe, intelligent design, or morality
2) <u>Pantheism</u> – belief that God is the universe
   a. Refutation
      i. Fails to explain existence of evil
      ii. Reincarnation needs physical bodies & individual souls
      iii. If God is unknowable, how could we know pantheism is true?
      iv. Can't live like the world is an illusion
      v. No reason to be moral
3) <u>Panentheism</u> – the universe is God's body
   a. Refutation
      i. God can't be both finite & infinite in His basic nature
      ii. A finite, changing God needs and infinite, unchanging God to ground its existence
4) <u>Deism</u> – God created the universe, but doesn't intervene
   a. Refutation
      i. Creation is God's greatest miracle – why can't he perform lesser ones?
      ii. Laws of nature are descriptive, not prescriptive
      iii. God can supercede laws of nature

World Views (2)

5) <u>Finite godism</u> – God is limited because of evil
   - a. Refutation
     - i. A finite god needs and infinite Cause
     - ii. A finite god doesn't deserve worship
     - iii. A finite god can't guarantee evil is defeated
     - iv. Evil does not prove God is limited
6) <u>Polytheism</u> – many gods
   - a. Refutation
     - i. Several gods would limit each other
     - ii. Limited beings need and unlimited cause
     - iii. Lesser gods = demons
7) <u>Theism</u> – the belief in a personal God
   - a. Transcendent – beyond the universe
   - b. Immanent – involved with the universe
   - c. The only world view supported by the evidence

Atheism

1) <u>God</u> – no God

2) <u>Creation</u> – no creation; either universe
   is eternal or it came from nothing

3) <u>Bible</u> – merely a human book with errors

4) <u>Salvation</u> – no life after death

5) <u>Jesus</u> – merely a man; not God, not
   savior, no miracles

6) <u>Man</u> – an evolved animal; mere
   molecules in motion

7) <u>Sin</u> – no such thing as sin

8) <u>Morality</u> – usually – moral relativism

9) <u>Truth</u> – usually – no absolute truth

Christianity

1) God – one personal God who is 3 persons
2) Creation – God freely chose to create the universe out of nothing
3) Bible – God's inerrant Word & the ultimate authority for our beliefs & behavior
4) Salvation – by God's grace alone, through faith alone, in Jesus alone (not by works)
5) Jesus – God the 2nd person of the Trinity, became a man, died on the cross for our sins, rose from the dead, will return
6) Man – created in God's image, human life is sacred, man is fallen & needs to be saved
7) Sin – we are all sinners who need to be saved
8) Morality – God's absolute moral laws
9) Truth – absolute truths exist

<u>Judaism</u>

1) God – one personal God
2) Creation – God freely chose to create the universe out of nothing
3) Bible – Old Testament is God's Word; New Testament is not.
4) Salvation – through obedience to God's law & devotion to the God of Israel (no substitute sacrifice)
5) Jesus – just a man; not God, not Savior, not Messiah
6) Man – human life is sacred; man was created in God's image; not now perfect
7) Sin – we are all sinners but can earn salvation through repentance & good works (no substitute sacrifice)
8) Morality – God's absolute moral laws
9) Truth – absolute truths exist

Islam

1) God – one personal God

2) Creation – God freely chose to create the universe out of nothing

3) Bible – Bible & Koran are God's Word; Koran is later & therefore superior

4) Salvation – through obedience to Allah's Laws & devotion to Him. (No substitute sacrifice)

5) Jesus – a great prophet, but Mohammed is greater; Jesus is not God or Savior.

6) Man – human life is sacred; man was created in God's image; not now perfect

7) Sin – we are all sinners, but can earn salvation through repentance & good works

8) Morality – God's absolute moral laws

9) Truth – absolute truths exist

<u>3 Main Theistic Religions</u>

1) <u>Judaism</u>

   a. Christ fulfilled their OT prophecies (they deny this)

   b. Devolved into salvation by human effort (no substitute Sacrifice)

   c. Refuted through historical apologetics (Christ's deity & resurrection)

2) <u>Islam</u>

   a. Many contradictions in Koran

   b. Teaches salvation by human effort

   c. Refuted through historical apologetics (Christ's deity & resurrection)

3) <u>Christianity</u>

   a. Teaches salvation by God's grace (substitute Sacrifice) (Eph. 2:8-9; Mt 19:25-26)

   b. Confirmed by historical apologetics

   c. Superior to other theistic religions

      i. God's justice & holiness

      ii. God's love & grace

      iii. Christ's substitutionary death

Hinduism

1) God – impersonal god is the universe (pantheism & polytheism)

2) Creation – no creation; universe is eternal; physical universe is an illusion

3) Bible – bible is not God's word; Bagavad Gita & other Hindu scripture (Vedas/Upanishads)

4) Salvation – reincarnation, meditation, devotion to Guru, all faiths lead to God

5) Jesus – one of many manifestations of God

6) Man – man is god, impersonal

7) Sin – no such thing as sin

8) Morality – moral relativism

9) Truth – no absolute truth

Buddhism

1) God – agnostic or same as Hinduism

2) Creation – no creation; universe is eternal

3) Bible is not God's word; teachings of Buddha are

   superior

4) Salvation – reincarnation, meditation, 4 noble

   truths, 8 fold path

5) Jesus – a guide & great moral teacher, not God,

   not the Savior

6) Man – man is impersonal

7) Sin – no such thing as sin

8) Morality – moral relativism

9) Truth – no absolute truth

New Age Movement

1) God – impersonal god; god is the universe

2) Creation – no creation; universe is eternal

3) Bible – occult experiences are ultimate authority

4) Salvation – reincarnation, meditation, new age on earth

5) Jesus – one of many manifestations of god – not savior

6) Man – man is God; impersonal

7) Sin – no such thing as sin

8) Morality – moral relativism

9) Truth – no absolute truth

Philosophy of Religion
Course Overview—Dr. Fernandes

1) introduction (what is philosophy, religion, religious experience?)

2) the relationship between faith & reason

3) world views

4) the case for theism (arguments for God's existence)

5) the problem of religious language

6) the problem of evil

7) the attributes of God

8) the possibility of miracles

9) God & history (Creation & Fall; nation of Israel; historical Jesus; resurrection)

10) God & redemption (incarnation, atonement, the Trinity)

11) life after death & the soul

12) religious pluralism (pluralism, inclusivism, universalism, exclusivism)

13) religion & science

14) God & morality (ethics)

15) history of philosophy (Justin Martyr, Origen, Augustine, Anselm, Aquinas, Bonaventure, Descartes, Pascal, Paley, Kierkegaard, Kant, Hegel, Hume)

Philosophy of Religion

--introduction

--faith & reason

--world views

--postmodernism

--religious experience

--religious language

--problem of evil

--traditional arguments for God

--the cumulative case for God

--science & religion

--history & religion

--pluralism, hell, Old Testament genocide, etc.

--philosophical theology (incarnation, atonement, Trinity)

<u>Seven Basic World View Questions</u>
(James Sire—*The Universe Next Door*)

1) What is prime reality—the ultimately real?

2) What is the nature of external reality—the world around us?

3) What is a human being?

4) What happens to a person at death?

5) Why is it possible to know anything at all?

6) How do we know right and wrong?

7) What is the meaning of human history?

The Ontological Argument

1) The greatest conceivable being must have every possible perfection
2) Existence is a perfection
3) The greatest possible being must have existence

1) All being is either necessary (cannot not exist) or possible (able to exist or not exist)
2) Impossible being cannot exist
3) It is impossible for necessary being to be possible being
4) A necessary being must exist

1) The greatest possible being must exist in all possible worlds
2) The actual world is a possible world
3) The greatest possible being must exist in the actual world

The Teleological Argument
(the argument from design)

1) Specified complexity/complexity of life (Dembski; Hoyle & Wickramasinghe)

2) Irreducible complexity (Michael Behe)

3) Anthropic principle (fine-tuning of universe)

4) Guidance of mindless nature/natural laws (Aquinas)

5) Anticipatory design (A. E. Taylor)

6) Logos—the coherence of the material world

7) Earth—designed for discovery

The Moral Argument for God's Existence

1) all humans make moral value judgments.

2) the moral law does not come from each individual since we condemn the actions of other individuals (i.e., Hitler).

3) the moral standard does not come from each society because we often condemn the actions of other societies (i.e., Nazi Germany).

4) the moral standard does not come from any world consensus since we often condemn the world consensus—even moral relativists try to change the world for the good (i.e., slavery, human rights, women's rights, etc.).

5) we appeal to a moral standard above all individuals & societies, and any world consensus.

6) when we condemn the actions of the past we imply the moral standard does not change with time.

7) since the moral law is prescriptive & not descriptive, there must be a moral law giver.

8) this moral law stands above all individuals and societies, and any world consensus.

9) this moral law giver does not change with time.

Dealing with Moral Conflicts

--unqualified absolutism

--conflicting absolutism (lesser evil)

--graded absolutism (greater good)

--<u>my view</u>—unqualified minimal absolutism

Cumulative Case for God

--theism treated as a hypothesis (the best explanation of the data)

--preponderance of the evidence (51% probability)

--theism is more reasonable as an explanation

--<u>common aspects of human experience</u>
- --beginning of the universe
- --continuing existence of the universe
- --moral experience
- --design in the universe
- --absurdity of life without God (meaning in life; hope)
- --validity of human reason
- --human rights
- --human free will & responsibility
- --self awareness
- --guilt
- --existence of evil

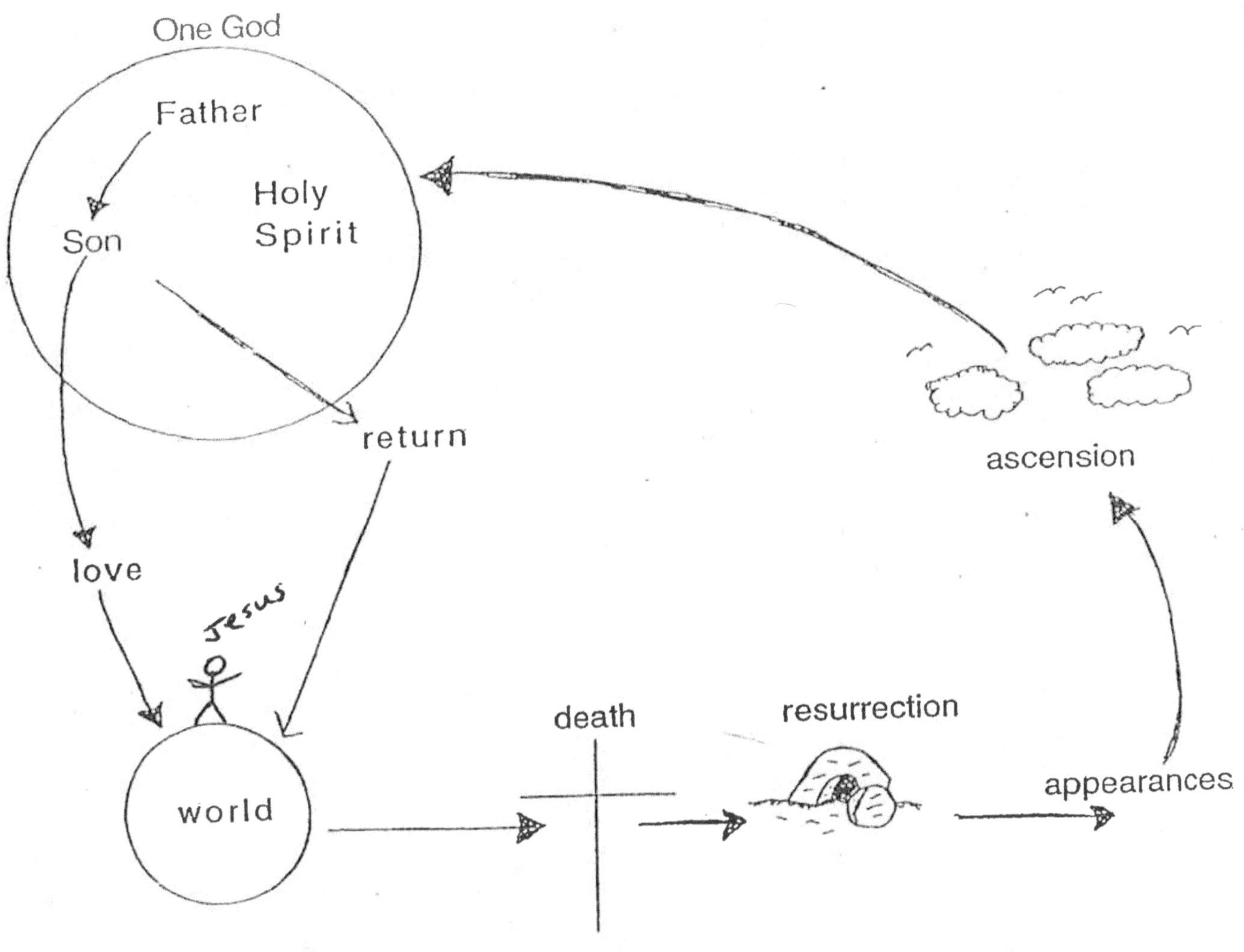

10 Gospel Truths

1) only one God
2) God is 3 Persons
3) God the Father loves the world
4) God the Father sent His Son into the world
5) God's Son became a man
6) He died on the cross for our sins
7) He rose from the dead on the third day
8) He appeared to His disciples
9) He ascended to heaven
10) He will return someday

Our Threefold Response

1) admit we are sinners & we cannot save ourselves
2) trust in Jesus alone for salvation
3) trust in Jesus & His Word for daily living

www.ingramcontent.com/pod-product-compliance
Lightning Source LLC
Chambersburg PA
CBHW080303030726
47593CB00009B/2610